We W
Nobbut G

Memoir of David Whitaker Gardner

KATHARINE ANN ANGEL

Foreword

These are the memories of me, David Whitaker Gardner, as related to my daughter-in-law Katharine. Over 4 years, I've recalled bits of my life story, piecing together events from the *olden days* until today, July 2016. Of course, aged 84, you'll understand that my mind will have fuzzed a few of the facts, but this is not deliberate, and if in places you disagree with my recollections, I beg forgiveness. Family and friends may differ in their version of who said what and what happened when, but I've done my best to be truthful, as a straight northerner should be.

    This all began after Anne had died. I was telling my life story to our friends David and Liz Ollerton. As we sat in my front room they said, 'Why don't you write this down as it is quite a story?' When I told Katharine I was writing my own story she was very interested and said, 'Show me what you've done so far,' so I did – but after all my efforts and despite my enthusiasm, I could only hand her a single page of handwritten notes! Katharine said, 'Let's work on this together - you can speak it out and I'll type as you talk.'

    Eight decades is witness to much history, as a family, as a business and in the world. Here are mere snippets to inform you, maybe amuse you, and certainly to help you piece together the *who's who* of the Gardner clan. Today in 2016, my seven adult children are long since grown and married, living in London, Leicester, Cornwall and Lancashire. My sixteen grandchildren range in age from 4 to 32. My great-grandsons are Joel 5, Sam 4, Zeb 3,

Ethan 18 months and Jesse, new-born as this book goes to print, 8th October 2016. Also, Alex and Phil are expecting a baby in December.

Whatever else my family discover as they read this, my heart's desire is that they realise how deeply the roots of their lives delve into our family love for God. Through all my decision-making, my successes and failures, my strengths and weaknesses, my joys and sadnesses, faith and doubt, I only ask that readers know this: *God has been.* Ask Him, in the quietness of your soul, to be in your today. God is. The puzzle can be solved.

First, to my brother Peter

Special thanks to you, Peter, for keeping me straight all these years. I could try to make 2 + 2 equal 5, or 3, or whatever I willed, but you always insisted on the answer being 4. Out of love, you pensioned me off early because of my back problems, but you kept me involved by asking my opinion on business plans and decisions; even when I pastored in Cornwall, you rang regularly. Under your capable financial management and with your consistent Christian integrity, we ended up with depots at Greens Farm, Winmarleigh, then Caton Road and the subsidiary 20,000 square feet at Courtaulds, Caton Road which Jonny managed, then Howarth Bros., Ingleton and finally the largest site at Carnforth. In all our years of working together, you and I never had a serious disagreement. We were grateful to Ron Walker for his expertise in warehousing and management.

A Word from David Ollerton

My first memory of David is of the fast-moving grocer, wearing shorts and wide-rimmed Scout hat, rushing boxes of groceries to scattered farms. After the mission to Dolphinholme in early 1969, he became my private mentor. As soon as his shop closed I was at the side door with my list of questions arising from my reading of the Bible that day. At the same time, he opened the 'Upper Room' to young local Christians as well as converts of the mission, to study the Bible and pray and sing together. We all owe David and Anne a debt of gratitude for what this did for our lives. David was a wonderful influence and a restraint on our enthusiastic (sometimes wild!) excesses.

The seed of Christian faith that began in me at that mission has grown stronger and deeper all my life. My peace is 'In Him.' As the chemo wears off I am feeling fine and will walk on the Black Mountains tomorrow. This is not a reflection of how I really am. I won't know that until after a scan at the end of August. If this third chemo has not checked the spread or reduced the tumour, I am not quite sure what is next. Heaven in a year – or ten? That depends on what the Lord does, so we will just have to wait and see.

Throughout my life, David and Anne encouraged me with books, pictures, gifts, letters, not to mention chalet, caravan and villa – all came with the handwritten words: 'In Him' and 'Hebrews 13 v 8,' which sums David up quite nicely really.

A Word from Barrie Walton

One of my first recollections of David was not long after I had arrived at Pilling as the minister and with responsibility for Dolphinholme Methodist church where he and Anne and the family worshipped. A phone conversation went wrong, ending in a strong disagreement between two equally strong characters. I distinctly remember putting the phone down, thinking, "You've blown that one, Barrie. That's a bad start."

A week or so later I was at a circuit meeting and who should walk towards me but David. He greeted me with a broad smile and called me "brother Barrie". So began a wonderful friendship which has lasted fifty years and to this day is better than ever. We value it more than words could say. Over the years I have visited David's home many times and shared laughter and deep spiritual fellowship. On my ever first visit (1966) I saw 9-year-old Andrew changing Simon's nappy.

One day, the Gardner family invited me for tea. The whole family were assembled. On their best behaviour, I must add. Just as we were about to sit down David exclaimed "FHB!" I had no idea what that meant but soon found out it meant FAMILY HOLD BACK. Was I glad.

David's devotion to the Lord and the gospel as well as his family is wonderful. His love for the Lord is evident at all times. He has always wanted to serve. Eva and I have always admired his willingness to step in at the last moment without a complaint. And we thank the Lord that he continues to be our friend.

We Were Nobbut Grocers

What is it that farmers have against grocers? A farmer called Jonty Collinson from Gift Hall Farm, Winmarleigh, was over for a nosy and natter at Greens Farm as our smart red haulage wagons came and went. He leant on the fence and said in his broad Lancashire accent,

'You lads have done all reet for yersens, because you were nobbut grocers.' I don't know what it is that farmers have against grocers, because a Christian farmer friend said he'd prayed for a wife because he wanted to marry a farmer's daughter, but he said, 'I ended up with a grocer's daughter from Hornby!'

This is my story - at least as much as I can remember of it. I hope you'll think of it as simply a scrapbook, crammed with bits of yesterday's news cuttings stuck between anecdotes, each recalled as a black and white photo of yesteryear, or a colourful tale of today.

From grocer to great-grandfather,
From Dolphinholme to Gillows Green,
My story wraps around these words:
God has been.

I was born David Whitaker Gardner on 6th August 1932 at 6am, the second of three children to Harold Wilcock Gardner and Elizabeth Gwendoline Whitaker (Gwen). My sister Elizabeth, known as Betty, was aged four. Our address was The Stores, Dolphinholme, near Lancaster, Lancashire, but the area was Ellel. My mother

Gwen was born at Barker House, on 26th September 1902, (the date of the Battle of the Boyne in Ireland). Barker House is now a historical building within the renowned Lancaster University.

My dad, Harold, and his brother Eddie were the two children from the second marriage of my Grandad Joseph Gardner, (his first wife died). The six boys from Grandad Gardner's first marriage never really accepted his new wife, but their two sisters were fine with their new siblings, Harold and Eddie. One of those six sons, my Uncle Richard, was for some reason the most anti and the result of this antagonism was that my side of the family never got into any kind of healthy family relationship with Dad's step-brothers.

I don't remember my great-grandparents on either side. My maternal great-grandmother was Margaret Barker, who had been married twice. Her last name was SHAW. Her second marriage was to James Barker from Gunnerthwaite near Arkholme. As strong Methodists, they attended Arkholme Methodist Church and also held Sunday afternoon services in their farmhouse until about 2004. My grandmother was Elizabeth, and we called her Grandma Whitaker. After the death of her husband, Grandma Whitaker would go around to the homes of her sons and daughters staying with each in turn for a period of time, but mainly she stayed with us at the shop. And she was treated like a queen! In my mind's eye, I can see her sitting in a chair in front of a fire, in the kitchen of the stores, chewing her food and spitting it out again and putting it on the side of her plate. She had digestive problems – even now I can see the little piles of chewed up meat!

A very early memory

I was four years old when Dr Holmes removed my appendix and discovered that I had peritonitis which was a very dangerous operation in those days. One reason I remember it is because Mrs Owtram from Newlands Hall visited me and gave me Needlers Boiled Sweets. (We had jars of these on the shelves in the shop). Mrs Owtram was a lovely, gracious person who was a real lady of the village. I still have a big scar where my stomach muscles are knotted and hardened where my appendix had been removed. In my late fifties I developed a problem with pancreatitis. As I lay on the floor in the bedroom I thought I was going to die. The words 'This is it!' filled my mind. When they came to operate, because of the knotted muscles where my appendix had been removed, and possibly too much fat (!) the medics couldn't reach my pancreas the normal way. They tried two keyhole operations. They bored twice but eventually they gave up and cut my chest open instead.

'I never remember any wet days!'

I was brought up in my parents' Groceries and Provisions Shop which was also a post-office at Dolphinholme. We sold every type of grocery; flour, coal, paraffin oil for lamps as well as oil heaters and lamp glasses for different lamps. We sold Appleby's flour that came in 3lb, 6lb and 12lb lovely little linen bags all together in a large hessian sack. We sold yeast or barm as we called it in those days. We also sold comics and Women's magazines, as well as Farmer's Weekly which is still going today. Us kids used to read all the comics - Dandy, Beano, Victor - before we sent them out to customers. We kept them clean, of course! Once, a lady came into the shop and asked for her 'My Weekly' magazine- and I jokingly blurted out, 'My weekly, my monthly, my yearly!' The woman looked shocked. Later my father took me aside and explained what 'my monthly' really meant . . .

I was so happy - I never remember any wet days.

Yes, that's me!

Like most children at that time, I used to go outside all day and only come home for meals. I was a menace in the village, causing all manner of trouble. I often played 'Knock-a-door-run.' I had a pin and bobbin or a button on a piece of string which I'd use to chink away at people's windows to annoy them until they rushed out, infuriated. Once I covered myself with a sheet and knocked on Mrs Pearce's front door. When she answered I scared the living daylights out of her. Mr Pearce came to our front door with a strap in his hand and asked my mum, 'Where's David?' He wanted to whack me with his belt, but my mum said, 'I will deal with it.' I had dashed up the warehouse stairs to hide.

When I was 8 years old me and my friends, Bob Parkinson and Bill Winder, let out some ferrets that belonged to a neighbour, Mr John Willy Winder. Mr Winder marched around to *my* house (of course) and knocked at the door. Before he could tell my parents anything I blurted out, 'I didn't let your ferrets out, Mr Winder!'

Another time I threw a stone and broke a window in my Dad's shop. I didn't tell anyone, but in the morning I woke to see the local PC, Bill Matthews, standing at the bottom of my bed. I quickly confessed to the crime which was just as well because my mate Bill Winder had already told the policeman it was me. Nowadays I'd be handed an ASBO for all the 'crimes' I committed!

Whenever there was trouble, people automatically assumed it was me, but occasionally they were mistaken. Someone knocked at our house to complain to my parents after something had happened in the village, but I was on holiday at Birchenlea Farm in Colne atop a very steep hill called Lenches with my Uncle George and Aunty Pegg Kelsall and my cousin Gwen Moorhouse - so it couldn't have been me. I would be only 8 or 9 years old, taking the bus by myself to Burnley. Gwen would meet me off the bus and take me to a restaurant. She'd show me how to use knives and forks properly because she'd been to *'la-de-da'* Ackworth, which was a Quaker Girls' Boarding School. At the foot of the hill was the Methodist chapel they attended. I used to go and help Uncle George kit milk door-to-door - a milk kit or churn is a ten or twelve-gallon drum. Uncle George used to go around Colne with a couple of milk kits; we used to measure the milk into their jugs or whatever receptacle they'd put outside on the step and they'd get a pint or whatever they wanted.

One day, at the farm, I saw Uncle George neck an old hen and throw it straight into the pig sty. I can see the pigs gobbling at it even now - the hen kept flapping but the pigs made short work of it, feathers and all! That was when I learnt that pigs were carnivorous.

I stayed at Birchenlea Farm twice. On a family visit to the farm, my brother Peter, aged only nine years, fell into the midden. The midden was full of liquid cow manure and seriously he could have died, but very thankfully he was rescued. Talking of Peter, who is nine years my junior, I once hit him in the solar plexus and totally winded him. I thought he'd died, but thankfully he survived. A year or two after the war, it was discovered that Uncle George and

11

Aunty Pegg still possessed two tea-chests full of canned goods, most of which were rusty. They'd stocked up, just in case . . .

My older sister Betty was very often ill, usually with asthma and she missed much school. I used to come home from school and climb into bed beside her to play board games. I suppose her ill health must have been stressful for my parents because years later, when my mum got angina she said, 'Now it's my turn to be nursed.' My mum took to lounging around and resting a lot. My parents often argued, but as a family I remember some really special times. For example, every bank holiday Dad would take us all out for a meal somewhere. We'd cram into his classy Austin Westminster which could do about 65 or 70mph and head for Sedburgh or some such place. We once had dinner at the Black Bull in Sedburgh which cost the princely sum of about 5 or 6 shillings a head – quite something back then. It was a special treat for bank holiday Monday, and we all wore our Sunday best suits! This tradition continued until Peter and Marian got married and had children – then we'd take two cars.

We enjoyed traditional Christmases as we decorated the tree, the shop and the house and hung out a pillowcase for Father Christmas. In the morning there was always an orange, a walnut and an apple at the bottom of the pillowcase, along with some toys. It was Dad who would get me ready for Sunday school each week. He'd stand me in the slop stone (sink) to do my hair. If I dared to move he'd whack me with the back of the brush!

Teenage Times

When I was a young teenager our parents took us for a week to stay in a guesthouse in Llandudno, Wales. Betty and I rode donkeys on the beach. (Before Peter was born)

We children used to play freely in the woods. One day I went into the wood down near Latham's Farm where there was a small plantation of ash tree saplings, tall and spindly, like whips. I cut down about twenty of them and built a den in the garden in the shape of an igloo. This is definitely something I regret, because when you are young you don't consider the consequences of your actions.

A whole gang of us kids created a den in the shop garden, using a branch leant up against the wall that faced the entrance to the church. I'd light fires and cook all manner of food on it, bacon, sausage and what have you. The smoke wafted up through a hole in the wall next to the church. This was in the grounds where the old Congregational Chapel had been and the steps down to the boiler house were still there then.

13

This chapel was made of corrugated iron and was bought and turned into a social club for somewhere in East Lancashire. The district surveyor told my father, 'Don't think you'll ever get planning permission to build on this land.' I eventually turned the space into a beautiful garden with lawns and roses. (By the year 2000 there were two houses with garages built on this land, one of which is right up against the garden wall – far too close to it.)

No one worried about the safety of children in the way they seem to nowadays. Doors were never locked and bikes were left outside with no fear of them being stolen. Of course there were some odd men about. One such man came from a farming family. He lived with his mother four doors up from us. At night, he used to show bad pictures to young lads down in the school toilets. People knew about it but no one sent in the cavalry to pick him up! A second man was called Benny who lived in a cottage on Corless Mill Farm. He was a very innocent person but we children knew he wasn't quite 'all there.' He had a speech impediment and he'd stand around dribbling. We kids would go to Mill Woods, believing that Benny might be there and 'get us,' but of course nothing ever happened, and I'm very aware now of how mean we children must seem today.

From a young age, I loved the freedom of driving. Aged 15, without a licence of course, I delivered groceries around the houses and farms scattered over the area. If PC Bill Matthews was about, Dad would quickly walk up the Abbeystead Road to meet me, to take over the driving and stop me getting caught! Aged 17, I passed my test at the second attempt. On my first test, in our old van, I stalled the engine and the starter jammed, so I had to get out, put the vehicle in gear and rock the vehicle to release the starter. The examiner was sitting waiting in the van, while I rocked it, until I heard a click, and the starter was released. No wonder I failed. For my second test, PC Bill Matthews lent me his police driving manual which was a great help.

One night I was driving home from courting Anne when PC Matthews caught sight of me behind the wheel. In those days he used to come into our shop for a natter and a cup of tea with Dad as we sorted the Quernmore orders late at night. Over his brew he quietly said, 'I've seen *people* driving home at midnight, driving far too fast without stopping at the Give Way sign, just down at the Fleece Hotel corner.' I froze, but he said no more.

One of our customers was Old Man Charlie Pye who lived at Tarn Brook. I'd deliver his groceries and he'd be sat in his armchair by the fire. I'd knock at the door which was that ill-fitting that a cat could crawl under it and a bird could fly in over it! I'd walk in with the grocery box and unload it all onto their table. Charlie Pye would eat 'twist' (tobacco) chewing it over and over, and then, because he couldn't swallow the juices, he'd spit them into the fire. They shot past us like flying egg yolks. He never missed the fire and we heard every spit sizzle! It was a bit like Indians who eat betel nut and spit it into spittoons on the train station platform. I think the betel nut has some kind of aphrodisiac effect on them.

One Christmas, Dad and I delivered groceries to Bonnie's at Foxhouses. She offered us some Christmas cake and a large glass of raspberry wine which she swore was not alcoholic. All the same, I was glad of the cake as it helped the wine down! I was driving home and said to Dad, 'That stuff was strong - my leg is shaking on the clutch.' Betty remembers us returning home semi-intoxicated. So there you have it; I was driving home under the influence.

Then there was the lovely Graham family. When we delivered their groceries the kids, particularly Tommy, got so over-excited they'd jump up onto the table to unpack the boxes so we didn't have to do it. The bacon and other supplies flew everywhere! One day Margaret Graham was in our shop leaning against the counter because she was heavily pregnant, when Dr Reardon came in. He put his hands on her stomach and said, 'Still there then! They breed like rabbits up at Ortner.'

Mr and Mrs Blezard owned the whole of Dolphinholme Top Rows. She was a tyrant. Her husband never worked. They survived off the proceeds from all the rent from Corless Cottages. I had an old Primus stove which was a bit of a dragon because it sprayed burning paraffin everywhere. I decided to cover the end wall of the toilets and coal houses in flame from that Primus. Mrs Blezard's back door was opposite the toilets. I then knocked on her door so she saw her toilet wall was on fire!

She was furious, shouting and yelling and doing her usual. My sister Betty has since explained to me that the big risk was that in the next door building was a 500-gallon tank that stored the paraffin oil, which Dad sold for people's lamps and heaters.

However, I did learn something useful from the Blezards. Mr Blezard had prostate problems and no wonder – he sat all day by the fire with a bottle of beer next to him. His wife explained his prostate problem using information she'd got from the doctor; 'You know when you go to the toilet, and you could always do a bit more wee, well, my husband never drained himself out properly, so that's why he's suffering.' So because of her saying this, I have always drained myself out fully, and it must have worked because I have never had any problems with my waterworks - yet.

At times, I could be creative in a positive way. For example, we used to get butter in square wooden boxes with a lid that was wired on. When I was 15 years old, I used a hammer and a knife to turn one of these butter boxes into a garage for my younger brother Peter. I even put a light inside it, attached to a battery, with a switch and the lid of the box acted as a forecourt of the garage. I made a ramp onto the roof so Peter could drive his cars up and park them on the roof. Years later, I repeated this expertise when I made another garage using similar materials, to make a Christmas present for my primary school-aged sons, Timothy and Andrew. They loved it and played with it constantly.

1940 The War

I was only eight years old when war broke out; the beginning of rationing and a restricted situation. It made everyone resilient and inventive. As children we started collecting rosehips from the hedgerows and taking them to school. A chemical company then bought these hips from the school to make rosehip syrup and other products. Fruit was rationed and we never saw bananas. It was a treat at Christmas to have Jaffa oranges. Of course we had our own apple and plum trees, which was good. One day, my mum went to pick the plum trees and realised Connie Dodd had been in and pinched them. Connie was a real character. She was a married woman who'd laugh at all sorts of things. In the village shop, I overheard her talking to someone about some bloke and she said, 'Oh, he's far too fat, he couldn't get near me!' What was she going on about, I wonder?

During the war farmers received permits for extra rations for lambing time, hay-time and harvest-threshing (Johnny Ball from Hollins Lane would bring his threshing machine with a steam-engine and a belt from the engine would driver the thresher.) This was good for us because the farmers always took their full permit, probably more than they'd have bought anyway, and we were able to order more cheese, butter, margarine, lard and sugar into the shop. It was impossible for us to comprehend how hard it was for folk in the wider world because the country folk had access to milk and eggs, plus the farmers sold lamb, beef and pork. Anyone at all could keep animals. A local man called Tom Winder went around to butcher pigs for anyone who wanted this doing.

Mrs Yates at Gilberton Farm always requested extra syrup and sugar from us. They stocked up with so much of it that when the war ended I said, 'Now Mrs Yates, you can have as much sugar and syrup as you like,' and she took me into her larder to show me that they had something like fifteen two-pound packs of sugar and a dozen or so tins of syrup.

Jonny Pye farmed with his brother, Slinger Pye, at Haythornthwaite. Jonny and his wife Jenny lived at Lower Lea, Tarn Brook. In his back yard he kept a pig in a sty. When Tom Winder came to slaughter his pig, he discovered that someone painted it red and they had to work hard to scrub the paint off. Allegedly, the Gifford lads and Jim Pye had painted the pig with red ruddle, the red iron ore used for marking and identifying sheep. Another thing that amused those lads was placing stones across the track so I would have to get out of my van to remove the stones to deliver the groceries. Most likely they were hiding behind the wall laughing at me.

Farmers used to buy cob salt and saltpetre, which they used to cure (preserve) their pigs. The saltpetre was rubbed into the ham-bone to stop the meat going bad. Slinger Pye always ordered two cobs of salt from our shop, just to be sure. He never cottoned on that when the salt struck, the meat couldn't absorb anymore. Most people would give us bits of bacon, but when we got bacon from the Pyes, there'd be half an inch of salt in the bottom of the pan. Incidentally, nowadays if you tried to buy saltpetre from a chemist in even small quantities, you would be severely questioned, because it is a component of gunpowder! As boys aged 10 or 11, we made fireworks with sulphur powder, saltpetre and iron-filings. We'd light the mixture with a match and it would go off like a firework. It wasn't controlled or contained in an actual firework, so it would just burn very brightly as the saltpetre and iron filings spat and sparkled.

*

Towards the end of the war, there was great excitement. Two bombs dropped on Fell Side Farm above Catshaw Fell. Fortunately, no one was killed. We kids all trekked up to see the craters and that's about as much of the war as we had.

During the war my dad was in the Home Guard and later joined the ARP (Air Raid Precaution) because it was easier for him. He was responsible for issuing gas masks and ensuring people weren't showing lights at night. Being in the Home Guard meant Dad had to sit up all night in the Greenbank area where the two great pipes of Thirlmere Aqueduct crossed. Our local name for this pipeline where it crossed the River Wyre was 'The Pipetrack Bridge.' This pipeline was protected by barbed wire – after all, the Germans invaders might have tried to destroy it, thereby cutting off the water supply to Manchester. It was a great adventure for us eight-year-olds to climb across this bridge, surmounting the twisted barbed wire. I doubt we were supposed to do that!

The underground piping to Manchester had developed leaks, so one day a major firm arrived to fix them. They lined the pipes with cement. The farmers had depended on these leaks to water their cattle, and when these suddenly dried up they had to provide alternative solutions to give their cattle a drink.

Pennine View, Dolphinholme, was a searchlight battery during the war – they had searchlights there which pointed to the sky so anti-aircraft people to see to fire at the planes that came over. Also, the light blinded the pilots temporarily. At Starbank, an area just above Dolphinholme, where a farmer named Mr Lothian lived, there was a camp for Italian prisoners. They worked on farms and other things. Nearby, in Wellington Woods there were 8 concrete buildings for storing equipment for army reserves. I remember one of them was full of snow-shoes, the sort with rackets underneath. When I was about 13 years old, I sneaked in and found out how dead it felt in there. It was a frightening place. After the war, the buildings were eventually emptied and left to crumble. Some farmers used them for storing hay. Nowadays, they are overgrown and a bit creepy.

The Light of War and Colour of Wonder

The Stable Yard in Dolphinholme belonged to my father. It had been stables for six horses and all the paraphernalia that were needed by them. Dick Winder, a local builder, rented most of the area, the other part of which was three garages for rent. Dick dumped a huge pile of rubble onto this land for use as hard-standing and other building needs. In those days there were no street-lights or light pollution. One dark evening, Dad took me to stand on the top of the rubble heap. Together we climbed high enough to see the fiery glare and eerie glow of the distant city of Liverpool that had been badly bombed. Another night, we once more climbed the rubble, but this time we looked north and saw some magnificent flashing lights filling the sky, red, emerald and gold. Together, we were witnessing the wonder of the aurora borealis, the Northern Lights.

After the War

Very few children lived in the village. Four boys, Bill Winder and Bob Parkinson who lived on the front row, then Henry and Sammy Driver who lived on the back row. The only three girls were Audrey Winder who lived on the front row, Joan Capon who stayed with the Driver family on the back row and Edith Coulthard, who lived at Rose Cottages near the Fleece Hotel. When the war ended and a 13-year-old girl called Anne moved into the area she was fresh interest for me. Anne was very much a townie but I was immediately attracted to her. Edith once told me that when she'd been travelling home from Sunday school in the same car as Anne, Anne had announced, 'To think David Gardner says he likes me!'

Anne's father, George, had died when she was about ten years old leaving his wife, Elizabeth Phillips, to care for Anne and her brother, seven-year-old Joe. After George died his family lived with 'Aunty Grace' in

Blackpool, but when Elizabeth found work as a 'live-in' housekeeper she left her son with Aunty Grace and took Anne, first to live and work in Cottam, Preston, then to Quernmore Park, a huge stately home for the gentry. Eventually they moved to Cinder Hill Farm, situated by the Fleece Hotel crossroads in Dolphinholme, to keep house for the councillor/farmer, Mr Philip Bateman. Later Mr Bateman allowed Joe to come to live with them as well.

Anne's parents, Elizabeth and George

Incidentally, when Mr Bateman died he made provision for Mrs Phillips, a council house at Bolton-le-Sands. The family attended the Congregational Church there where some relations of mine, the Towers family also went. Anne had a friend called Daphne Butterfield. On Sundays the pair would walk three miles to work at Lancaster Beaumont Isolation hospital because there were no buses. Once, they were walking along the A6 when a lorry drove past - the passenger was urinating out of the door and this hit both Anne and Daphne! Terrible.

Anne started to attend our chapel which is where I first saw her. It was 1946. I was 14 and had already left school and was working in the shop. I was a bit shy as far as girls were concerned - actually I don't know if I am correct saying that! I began to walk Anne home from Sunday school and other chapel meetings. We hit it off straight away. I suppose you could describe me as 'quite the romantic,' because while Anne was still in school (Greaves School, Lancaster) I used to write notes to her and leave them in a crack in our garden wall by the bus stop. My friend Bill Winder, who was still attending school, would pick them out and take them to Anne in class. He would return with notes from Anne. When Anne had been cooking buns or pastries in class, she would send Bill back with some of her baking for me. One of her notes was a parody of a ditty of the time – *I'd love to climb an apple tree and sit on David Gardner's knee. I know it really shouldn't be. It's naughty, but it's fun!* and so it went on . . .

Through our mid-teens I was often working in the evenings, so I would ring Anne (our shop phone number at Dolphinholme was Forton 240). Anne would make some excuse to her mother before walking over the fields to meet me at the gateway on Four Lane Ends for quarter of an hour. Some Sundays we'd both cycle to Nicky Nook, then pedal back via Scorton to buy an elicit ice-cream (*well, it was the Sabbath!*) from the van by the iron bridge. One day, Anne got bicycle oil on her new full-length green coat, so we headed for Brindle and Pye's garage opposite the Fleece Hotel, where I cleaned her coat using petrol that was still in the pipe at one of the pumps.

The Most Wonderful Thing That Ever Happened

We were sixteen and I still wasn't bold enough to walk Anne home with my arm around her the way my friend David Close did with his girlfriend, Edith Coulthard. David was a confident character. I remember him going out with Anne's cousin Julie, walking beside Anne and I around Lancaster Castle. Julie was fairly tall so David had to sit on the wall in order to be the same height as her to kiss her. After two years of walking Anne home from church, one night we stopped by a corn-stack at Cinder Hill Farm and I asked Anne if I could kiss her. She said yes! It was the most wonderful thing that ever happened! After that, as I walked up Pennington Hill from the Fleece up to Dolphinholme, I kind of floated home.

We were not allowed to get married until Anne turned twenty-one. I went to see her mother to ask for Anne's hand in marriage and she spent twenty minutes telling me all the bad things about Anne, which I never did see. Looking back, maybe she was not being unkind, but trying to be realistic and making sure I was not just looking through rose-tinted spectacles.

School Days, Scouts and Army Boys

Betty ran to tell my mother I was being rude at Dolphinholme primary school because I deliberately walked around school with a piece of red wool through my flies like a little tail. My sense of humour was developing even as a youngster. Maybe this is the reason that as a young lad I wasn't clever enough to get into the grammar school, so my father decided to send me to what they considered to be the next best thing to a grammar, the Friend's School in Lancaster, a Quaker school by the station on Meeting House Lane. The head at Dolphinholme Primary was Mr Todd. In my last fortnight there, he caned me at every opportunity. He used to say, 'Gardner, you're not going to let me down when you go to that Lancaster school.' He used to cane any of us for getting things wrong. He once gave Dick Green a right good caning, after which Dick jumped over the school wall and ran home. And so I was sent to the *Friends' School* and my parents had to pay £15-25 a week for this privilege.

The headmaster at the Friends' School, Mr Drummond, was nicknamed Bulldog Drummond, after a character in a book. Bulldog Drummond wrote on my last report; *'If David doesn't improve, his position here is jeopardised.'* And the maths teacher told my parents, *'David is better at firing ink pellets than he is at doing maths.'* I thought that was rude because I'd done the best I could, so I told Dad, 'That's it. I am coming home to work in the shop.' I really wanted to be a mechanic because I fancied working on engines, but Dad's only intention was for me to work in the shop so I took the line of least resistance. At least I was getting out of school.

So I left school when I was 14, which you could in those days. Four years later, when I was in the army I got 96% in my medical exams in Cowglen Hospital, so I can't have been as thick as they'd made out. There, the Sister Tutor was so impressed she suggested I stay on in the army and become a teacher. She lent me a book called 'The

Glands of Destiny' - I loved reading about such things as the *pituitary gland* and the part it played in our lives. Regretfully I never gave her the book back and I had it for many years! But more about Sister Tutor later . . .

*

The scouting movement in the area was run by George Maddison who was a valet for the Vicar of Over Wyresdale. George was a Christian man from the Church of England. He wore dark horn-rimmed glasses and was a very likeable person. At the end of war, as a young teenager I joined the scouts. We hung out in a scout hut near the old gas mill chimney in Lower Dolphinholme. Later we moved to the Memorial Hall which gave us more space for activities especially when it was raining. Once, we'd begun to follow some written instructions on how to tie knots, when I noticed two lads sitting together with tears in their eyes. I asked them, 'What's the matter?' They replied, 'We cannot read.' So I said, 'I will show you.' These were the twins, Vincent and Brian Mullen, who despite their illiteracy at this stage, they grew up and did okay in the rest of their lives.

Soon after I'd married, I restarted the Scout movement in Dolphinholme. We had various adventures including a trip to Wray Castle, across Windermere from Ambleside. Ronald Kenyon was a livestock haulier (more about him later) who transported us all there in his cattle truck. Forget health and safety, Ronald chucked all the scouts and their tent equipment in the back of his truck and rattled us up to Wray Castle where we set up camp. We set to, digging channels around the green ridge tent to prevent rain running through, because there were no linings or ground sheets. For a communal eating area, we'd borrowed a big tent from my mother's double cousin, Uncle Joe Towers. Everyone in our church knew him as Uncle Joe because of our relationship with him.

I hired a boat at Wray Castle. Ten of us rowed (without lifebelts) over the water to Ambleside. On our way back, a thunder-storm started. The whole experience was terrifying. Lightening was everywhere, the water was choppy and the rain was so heavy that the droplets were bouncing up off the lake like diamonds. The boys all loved it and at the same time they were scared. When I think about it now, I never even asked those kids if they could swim. Nowadays of course, the cost of following Health and Safety standards would prevent this kind of adventure.

I haven't yet mentioned football. I played inter-village football for years. I finally hung up my boots aged 45, too old really but I enjoyed playing for our firm Safegard Storage in a local businesses five-a-side summer league. As a youngster on the village team we wore clogs on our feet – yes, the ones with wooden bases with iron caulkers and leather lace-up tops. (We sold these at the shop!) It was very painful if you got 'clogged' on the shin, or anywhere else for that matter. Eventually that footwear was banned. We played teams such as Whitechapel and Claughton-with-Brock, over Inskip way – and Ronald Kenyon would transport us in his cattle wagon!

I once, only once, fouled Twin (Tom) Harrison. He said, "Gardner, don't thee start summat you can't finish." I've repeated this to my grown-up grandsons many times, much to their amusement, and now they remind me, saying, "Grandad, don't start you can't finish."

*

When I was converted to Christianity, (a story I will tell you all about later) immediately I got grand ideas to be a missionary. Our chapel had strong connections with Cliff College so I thought, 'I've got to go to Cliff to study the Bible and become a church minister. I was only seventeen, so the college let me in with six other lads to work as cleaners as we studied. We polished the corridors with a big buffer thing, which swung from side to side as we did the floors. We cleaned toilets and emptied rubbish. We did everything that was needed. In exchange we were given two lectures and 25 shillings per week. We also accompanied the Trekkers as part of their team.

I went to Cliff College in early December and came home for Christmas, returning after the holiday. I think Anne wrote to me every day I was away. She was working as a nursery nurse on Willow Lane in Lancaster. In the July I went on the 'Lowestoft to Great Yarmouth' Cycle Trek. At the beginning of August, my father sent for me to come home because he was short of staff in the shop. I could never understand his decision, knowing I was going to have to join the army in September.

In those days it was obligatory for all the young men to do National Service. For me this meant spending two years in the army. A group of eighteen-year-olds went to Crookham Barracks in Aldershot for our initial basic training of eight weeks square-bashing, the military drill performed repeatedly on a barrack square. I was 'kind of' a conscientious objector but I realised I had to support my country so I joined the Royal Army Medical Core - RAMC *(known by many as 'Rob All My Comrades' because the RAMC were believed to take valuables off fallen comrades, or badly wounded comrades in the field)*. My aim was still to become a missionary and I knew the medical training would be an asset for this. I had to fill in a form which asked, 'What is your present job?' I wrote *Ministerial Candidate* and people assumed I wanted to be a politician and ended up explaining, 'No, I mean I'm training to be a Methodist minister.'

The first night in the barracks I knelt by my bed to pray. One lad told me, 'There was an older soldier in our last barracks who told lads who prayed, "You'll soon be cured of that. We threw boots at the last lad that prayed!"' Another man from the Salvation Army decided it was safer to pray *in* the bed than kneel beside it. No one ever threw boots at me.

The doctors who oversaw our health were definitely suspicious of anyone who presented with illness or pain. One time I suffered with a very bad back; even so I was forced to carry coal for a staff sergeant. I was weeping with pain but was told, 'Get on with the job.' Eventually they decided to send me to hospital in Camberley. After a few days, my back was suddenly better so I said to the doctor, 'I'm all right now.' He raised an eyebrow and said with sarcasm, 'That's amazing, Gardner,' so I knew he'd not believed me in the first place.

While I was on the ward with my bad back, half a dozen soldiers had to be given antibiotics for some reason. The nurse said, 'Line yourselves up.' The lads stuck out their bottoms all in a row to get the injections, then the nurses slapped them with one hand and stuck the needle in with the other! I got to do this job when I was helping out! Can you imagine? *Me giving injections!*

After basic training in Aldershot, there were choices of courses to go on. I chose hygiene. I volunteered to do hygiene training to become a hygiene inspector. This included training for running field hospitals and army camp inspections in every department including the cookhouse. Six of us fully-qualified hygiene people were posted to Catterick in North Yorkshire. We were supposed to direct the General Duty Orderlies (GDOs) but there were none, so it was left to us to do the work of a GDO which meant emptying and cleaning out the grease traps outside the hospital kitchens. These traps were similar to a sewage system with a small catchment area so the grease didn't leak into the drains. It was a filthy job. We took a cart around the married quarters and emptied their dustbins, taking the rubbish to a dump. I became so bored and fed up with Catterick that I volunteered to go to Korea! That shows I had no idea what I was doing. I mean, what would Anne have thought if I'd run off to war for some excitement? But eventually I did get posted to somewhere completely different – the wilds of bonny Scotland.

Each Friday night a bus was provided to go to Liverpool to take lads home on weekend leave. Many of the boys hailed from Liverpool so I would get on one of those buses and hop off at Lancaster where Dad would meet me. Then, at midnight on the Sunday night, I'd catch the bus at Greyhound Station in Lancaster to return to Catterick.

A trip was arranged by the army to go and visit the Queen's Jubilee Celebrations in London. The person who'd invited me to go was Sergeant Trinder. (The man turned out to be homosexual which obviously I had no idea about at the time). I was naïve – it had never crossed my mind until I got teased by the lads on my return. There was a lad from Middlesborough with a big, fat beaming face - beaming that is, until I called him a Geordie. He mocked me saying, 'Come on, tell us, how did you get on with Sargent Trinder?' I'd had no idea that Trinder might have been trying to groom me.

The Beginning of my Life-long Love and Attachment for Scotland

Initially I was posted to Cowglen Military Hospital in Glasgow. I was 18 years old. As we checked in at Cowglen guardhouse, a group of us were immediately told, 'You're on duty tonight.' There was a social problem because the Gorbals slum area in Glasgow was being redeveloped, but the 'girls of the night' were not being rehoused and were desperate for anywhere to stay. The redevelopment was ideal for the tenants of the new buildings because it was the first time they had baths in their homes. Some had absolutely no idea what to do with a bath so they kept coal in it and used the bathroom doors for firewood. Many new apartments became a mess and quickly deteriorated. *You can change the environment but not so easily alter hearts and habits.*

Some of the army lads enjoyed this job because 'guard' meant keeping the prostitutes out of the cabins that were not being used and they were often invited in for a 'cup of tea'! When my mate Alan Williamson was on duty at night Sister Tutor kindly left her premises open for Alan to use and instead of doing his 2 hours on and 2 hours off guard duty, he used to sleep through the night. I'd met Alan Williamson from Appleby when we were in Glasgow. He was an organist in the Methodist church at Appleby and his father was the manager of the Nat West Bank there. Another lad joined us from Northern Ireland who claimed to be a Methodist, but was more of an Orangeman. He was in my class, preparing for the medical exam. Another lad in our set was a clever young man, aiming for Leeds University, yet I gained 20 more marks than him because I concentrated and enjoyed the course so much.

The aforementioned Sister Tutor was the matron in charge of Cowglen Hospital. She suggested I should stay on and become a teacher. She also declared, 'No one leaves Cowglen without getting a medical three exam pass. You are in the RAMC (Royal Army Medical Core).' I passed my exams and was transferred to a medical reception centre on Strathern Road, Edinburgh, near to Arthur's Seat and Holyrood. There was a small ward with a big, fat major in charge, with male nurses and GDOs (General Duty Orderlies) to keep the place clean. One of the GDOs was a bookies runner for the station. He was a Roman Catholic from the Gorbals in Glasgow. When I shared my faith with him he wasn't at all happy about that. He warned me, 'Listen Gardner, if a priest told me to cut your throat I would do it!'

There was an ambulance base at Strathern Road, where we were on call, but the only reason I ever went out in the ambulance was to drive the mile to the fish and chip shop. The ambulance was a big, square affair. When we drove it we'd tie a bandage onto the outside and add flashing lights as if we were going to an emergency.

I went on hygiene inspections to different army barracks riding my motorbike, a 350 BSA Sidevalve engine on which I travelled as far as Berwick-upon-Tweed to inspect the army camp. It was a lovely run down the coast on the A1. I worked as a hygiene inspector of toilets and kitchens. I'd check for things like cracked cups and clean washing facilities. After all, hygiene in battle was a vital policy, especially concerning the latrines. I'd already completed six weeks' hygiene training because cleanliness in hospitals and kitchens was of the utmost importance. For field hospitals we were shown how to make a burner for destroying diseased garments, using diesel oil and water. You get the burner going with the oil, then add tiny drops of water which burn fiercely and the heat kills all the germs.

Rattus Rattus

Those terrible rats can get through the tiniest of spaces. They are easily recognised by their large translucent lugs! But I could dispose of them. The NAAFI had built a store on what had been an old corporation rubbish tip just outside Edinburgh and they were plagued with rats. I was the hygiene guy so I made it my job to check that the food was stored high on the palettes. Rats only need a hole big enough to poke your finger through

and they are in, because their skulls collapse – and the gap beneath each palette was 8cm! So, a group of men and I moved the palettes out then created a roughly circular trap using boards. Half a dozen rats rushed into this space so we proceeded humanely (!) to club these rats to death with spades. One of the beasts decided to head for daylight, just as one of the men ran for the doors. He was petrified, imagining this little rat was chasing him! Afterwards we cleaned up the carnage, and stocked everything higher up on the palettes. For several weeks afterwards I followed this work up by regular visits, baiting and baiting until no rats survived.

What more rats? The WRACS (Women's Royal Army Core) were billeted at the Carlton Hotel, Edinburgh. The hotel is on the North Bridges, at the end of Princes Street which leads up towards the Royal Mile. They had an infestation of rats, so my commanding officer sent me to sort it out. I persuaded him to let me book a room at the top of the hotel so I could stay until the rats were cleared. While living there, all I had to do was to bait rats.

They should have made me a corporal or sergeant really, but I was made a lance corporal. My job included suggesting that a cracked cup be thrown out or that a toilet needed cleaning, but the sergeant in charge of the cookhouse would often yell, 'Have I to obey instructions from you, a lance corporal? Not on your nelly!' to which I replied, 'If you're not happy with me, go and talk to your commanding officer.' End of argument.

At weekends those of us not attached to wards would be off duty. Charlotte Street Chapel reached out to support the army lads and at weekends, a lovely family called the Beverages who lived on East Preston Street allowed three or four of us to stay with them. We slept on the floor. They gave us food too. Sunday evenings we'd finish up with bread and syrup. In our youthful ignorance we didn't realise the cost to them of their generosity. Despite being away from home and Anne, the Beverages made those nine months in Edinburgh one of the happiest times of my life. Betty Beverage, one of the sisters in this family, was a midwife working in the Gorbals. She told us about a family from the Gorbals who'd invited her to share a meal with them. Betty said she guessed that family were Christians because they used 'clean' newspapers to cover their table. She often returned home exhausted from her work, and would put on the gramophone to play the hymn, 'O love that will not let me go.'

> *'O Love that will not let me go*
> *I rest my weary soul in thee;*
> *I give thee back the life I owe,*
> *That in thine ocean depths its flow*
> *May richer, fuller be.'*

I can see her now, the gramophone on the table and her sitting with her head in her hands, eyes closed, taking in the words and the meaning. She was a lass who, when having a meal with one of these families, if she found a grub in her salad she quickly ate it so she didn't hurt their feelings. She was such a good woman and God knows all about that.

Carrubbers Close Mission

The lads who came to East Preston Street tenement were Alan Williamson, Reg Eastup, Dennis Fox from Leeds and myself. On Sundays we'd go to hear Sidlow Baxter in Charlotte Street Chapel just off Prince's Street where I was eventually baptised.

It was typical of the Baptists in those days that about fifteen people were baptised together. I don't think I really appreciated what was happening and sometimes I wish I could get baptised all over again so I could really understand and mean what I was doing. At night we'd go to Carrubbers Close Mission on the Royal Mile which is still going strong today as a modern, lively independent evangelical church. Even in those days, there were always hundreds of people attending.

Charlotte Street Chapel

Sidlow Baxter led the Thursday night Bible Studies which were published as the popular *'Explore The Book.'* One of these evenings Sidlow said, 'Friends, I have composed a new tune to 'What a Friend we have in Jesus' – will you sing it for me?' and we sang as he played the piano. When Sidlow Baxter was leaving Charlotte Street to go to America he preached on Jesus' words, 'Oh Jerusalem, Jerusalem, how often have I longed to gather you as a hen gathers her chicks but you would not . . .' He spoke with tears in his eyes because of the hard heartedness of some of the leaders.

Each Friday night the revival prayer meeting was attended by fourteen people, four of whom were soldiers, yet in Charlotte Street Chapel they had a forty-strong choir. What I'm saying is that the choir was better attended than the prayer time. The choir conductor was the organist. She had a big nose and we used to call her a witch, because to us, that is how she looked. *(What a lovely Christian outlook we had – hmm!)*

On Tuesday nights we held open-air meetings on The Mound, a road near the art gallery at the centre of Princes Street. The Mound was similar to the soap box on Speaker's Corner on Hyde Park – anyone could stand there and shout their opinions or beliefs to passers-by. One of our men used to get up and shout, 'We are not Sad-u-cees, we are Glad-u-sees!' One night, a man called Bill Burts was passing. He heard us shouting Bible texts and simply through that, he became a Christian! He was almost illiterate but within a month he could read his Bible. Bill had been adopted by parents who ran a fair. He'd arrive in Edinburgh with the advance party, putting the posters up advertising the coming fair. Each year they visited Edinburgh he was always drawn to The Mound. (Some years afterwards, he married and continued as a Christian, even calling in to visit me in Dolphinholme.)

Some of the attitudes between so-called Christian groups who preached on The Mound could be appalling. For example, there was both a Catholic Truth Society and a Protestant Truth Society. The Protestants would stand up and say, 'The zoo has come to town and some of the monkeys have escaped but we know where they are – the Catholics over there!'

Our group of friends once went to Glasgow to do what we called 'open air work' in Sauchiehall Street. This was Glasgow's red-light district. A man in a raincoat and trilby came up to me asking for a word with me. I thought he was inquiring about faith but I was mistaken. He sounded accusing as he said, 'Why are the girls in your group not wearing hats?' I replied, 'Oh, you must be a

Brethren, are you?' I tried to explain about cultural settings. For some strange reason our gang attended a Brethren meeting at Portabello, just outside Edinburgh. We lads thought it was great because boys were allowed to sit at the front and speak, but the girls had to sit at the back and keep quiet!

Alan Williamson, who I mentioned before, was posted to the Redfern Barracks in charge of the medical centre. He became a lifelong friend and played the organ at our wedding. His parents had hoped he would become a doctor, but he saw so many what he called 'whingers' or malingerers - soldiers faking illness to get out of training that it put him off and Alan decided to become a vet instead. One day, whilst I was on hygiene inspection at Redfern I looked Alan up and he told me that a lad on TA training who was from Lewis and had been converted in the revival, had asked to meet for prayer. I was asked to join them. When he came he asked if he could pray in Gaelic because it was an easier language for him. To my Lancashire ears it sounded like someone speaking in a heavenly language.

When it was time for the Tattoo, I had to inspect the army barracks at Edinburgh Castle. In the dormitories, the bunk-beds were four men high and only a metre apart. Each man is supposed to have sufficient space but these men were packed like sardines and I was supposed to report these terrible conditions. However, their officer said to me, 'You can forget your inspection today,' and I had to walk out. The situation was just for the tattoo. All these different forces came to Edinburgh from all over the world and they had to be billeted somewhere, even though there was insufficient room to swing a cat.

1952 Skye

I was still in Edinburgh when it was time to take a short break with some army leave. Dad let me borrow his Austin which was marvellous of him! I had a good friend from Widnes called Reg Eastup who was in the RAF, stationed near Edinburgh Airport. Reg always called me Davy. Reg and I took our girlfriends, Joan and Anne, on a trip to Skye. Skye appeared to be such a small island that we imagined we'd be going off it every day, but we couldn't afford the ferry to leave the island at £5 a time. We all stayed at a B&B on the harbour at Portree. For some reason one day Anne and I argued. Because of this argument, I think Reg and Joan thought our relationship wouldn't last. Sadly, after they married, it was Reg and Joan whose relationship ended. One day we were walking on a hill when Anne slipped and fell and sprained her wrist. I drove us all to the hospital at Broadford and Anne ended up wearing a sling for the remainder of the holiday.

Another tale of army leave:
There were some girls at Kinlochleven who wanted to come to the church meeting. I persuaded the pastor to lend me his old Austin 8 car to pick up these girls and return them from the meeting. This I did, but I drove far too fast. Negotiating the bends round Loch Linne, the girls sang in the back happily and loudly, 'We're going to glory soon!' while I was thinking, 'You just might the rate I'm driving!'

Anne and I

I might have already said that Anne arriving in the village had sparked an interest for me. One of the other girls from Dolphinholme, Audrey Winder, married Bill Corless. a driver trainer in the RAF. Anne had failed her driving test first time, so Bill offered Anne lessons. He made her back around the corner at Ellel quarry at least a dozen times so she passed her second test with flying colours. She then used to drive the delivery van!

November 5th 1954, Anne and I were married in Dolphinholme Methodist Church and the reception was held in the Sunday School room, catered for by Olivers of Lancaster. The cost was

about seven shillings and sixpence per head. My childhood friend Francis Towers was my best man. Anne was living with her mother in Church Close, Bolton-le-Sands. Francis had lived on Broadlands Drive, less than half a mile away from Anne and her mother, so he looked after Anne for me while I was in the army. In fact, he used to take her out for rides on his motorbike to Stepping Stones at Silverdale. Naturally I was a little bit jealous but I knew Francis well, and above all I knew my Anne!

The wedding day had to be set on a day that didn't clash with what we called 'Quernmore week'- which happened every other week. Once a fortnight we delivered groceries around Quernmore which meant putting the orders up at ten or eleven o'clock at night. November 5th turned out to be a wet day meaning most of the photos were taken indoors. Before the ceremony something stressful happened: Frances and I were about to leave for the big event but we could not find the wedding ring anywhere. We hunted high and low, but we were not to know that my mother had moved it from its place in the desk to what she had thought would be a 'safe' place and we simply couldn't find it. As we stalled to hunt for it, the car taking Anne circled twice round Four Lane Ends and the Fleece Hotel. Finally, one of the caterers lent us her own wedding ring for the ceremony. All this time, Alan Williamson was entertaining the waiting congregation by playing the organ.

I was standing at the front with Francis waiting for the bride when I heard this sobbing and I thought it was my mother crying because she was losing her son. The sobbing landed beside me and it was Anne! She had been on nursing night duty for several weeks prior to the wedding, and with all the tension with the ring being lost, plus after seven years of courtship she was finally getting married to this wonderful man *(David says, 'Don't put that in Katharine!')* everything overwhelmed her. Anne stopped crying when I took hold of her hand. The Rev Gordon Mee married us. Gordon had been our superintendent minister for twenty years. He was a godly man with a face that shone. He always beamed widely. Anne and I spent the first night of our honeymoon in a hotel in Carlisle. As we travelled up there, we saw fireworks all around us. We walked into Central Hotel Carlisle with a travel rug over our arms as though it was something we had done all our lives and as we got to reception, the receptionist said, 'This is for you!' She handed us a long box labelled: *To the newly wed Gardners.* Inside was a poker, with some advice from the writer Bernard Shaw: *'When you get married, and your wife gets cross, pick up the poker and say, "I'm the boss."'* It had been sent by Malcolm Whitaker, my cousin from Gloucester. So our subterfuge was blasted. When we were in the lift, the girl who showed us to our room laughed, 'And don't you make a mess of our hotel bed tonight!'

The second and third night we spent in Oban then headed home, with only eighteen shillings in my pocket. We arrived at an upstairs apartment on the A6 at Cabus as tenants of Uncle Winder and Aunty Sarah Gardner. Uncle Winder was my dad Harold's step-brother. We stayed for six months until a lay-preacher/organist of Dolphinholme chapel, Mr Hogg, said he would help us find the money to buy a house. He took me in his big Wolsey car to see a solicitor in Castle Hill, Lancaster, and his driving was horrendous. That solicitor lent us £2000 from the exors of Mrs S Wright with which we purchased 'Vale View,' a semi in Dolphinholme, just above the chapel on Proctor's Corner. We renamed it 'Portree' after our first holiday destination in 1952. I was earning £6.50 per week at the shop working for Dad, while Anne was on

Feeding the turkeys at Portree with Timothy and Andrew

£6.75 per week as a fever nurse at Beaumont Hospital, Lancaster, so our joint income was £14.75 which was quite good in those days. We laid lino throughout the house because we couldn't afford carpets, except for one rug in the lounge. When the children eventually came along, they would take turns to play on this rug.

We struggled to pay the interest on the mortgage so I searched for a better paid job. I answered an advert from a book company that sold encyclopaedias. It was only when I was being interviewed I discovered this meant selling books door-to-door. The interviewer's opening gambit was, 'In this day and age with large classes in school, teachers cannot give independent tutorage to children and parents don't know all the answers, but by having these encyclopaedias to hand they can look up anything from A to Z.' I told him I was not interested in door-to-door selling. Days later, I was delivering groceries to one of our customers and caught sight of a pile of boxes full of encyclopaedias and I commented on them. The lady of the house replied, 'In this day and age with large classes in school, teachers cannot give independent tutorage to children and parents don't know all the answers, but by having these encyclopaedias to hand they can look up anything from A to Z.' I smiled but said nothing.

The First of Many Vehicles

Let me introduce you to our Morris Traveller we called 'Ofy.' This is the first vehicle we ever owned. It cost £300! I bought it with the profit from my turkey business. I kept a dozen turkeys at Portree, and had about 100 in the old mill building and then in the Stable Yard at Dolphinholme. I bought young chicks and fattened them for Christmas and sold them to the Co-Op.

We kept a hen with chicks in the greenhouse at Portree. One Sunday, on Harvest Festival, it rained so heavily that the greenhouse was flooded and we arrived home to find that the little chicks were literally floating in water. So we warmed our electric oven, then put the chicks inside it to dry them out - and they all survived.

Kraft Foods

We continued to live at Portree. At this time, I was preaching in the local Methodist church, never doing as much preparation as I should but I ad-libbed. I was also the Sunday school Superintendent which meant I organised the children to sing and recite things at anniversaries, which was the normal pattern of things in those days. Everything had a spiritual application.

In 1956 our second son, Andrew was born, not in hospital but in Portree, our house in Dolphinholme, so our family was growing and I needed more work in order to provide for them. I saw an advertisement for Kraft foods and thought, 'I can do that.' My interview took place in a big, white hotel, The Hydro in Blackpool on the North Shore. I got the job. This meant I had to cycle to Bay Horse to catch a bus or the train to Preston Station from where I'd walk the streets of Preston and Longton selling Kraft products, such as margarine and Dairy Lea cheese. There were plenty of customers. I had to visit 30 corner shops on New Hall Lane alone. One young grocer in Leyland took to me and he'd order 14 cases of margarine every time I called which, for me, was great.

Kraft Foods bosses reckoned that if they sold a dozen Dairy Lea to each shop that would amount to thirty dozen boxes of Dairy Lea on New Hall Lane, but of course that didn't work like that. No one counted on the shop-keepers separating the boxes of Dairy Lea to sell as individual triangles to cater for the local mill-workers, who only purchased a single triangle per day to put in a bread roll for their lunch. There were many foreigners, for example people from Pakistan, and other nationalities many of whom had moved in from Blackburn, all working in the mills. They tended to buy proper meals, because they worked hard and they needed it.

Many shop keepers just kept the shop because they could buy the food for their families wholesale from places such as James Hall of Preston and G&W Collins wholesalers. The health people did their rounds imparting new regulations regarding hygiene. They announced that all the shops must put in a sink with hot water for hand-washing, but many of the shopkeepers were unable to afford to comply with this rule and were forced to close down. This hit hard the extremely poor districts such as London Road.

Back at our Dolphinholme shop we were turning over £5-600 a week. I was always thinking of ways of increasing our income so listened hard when a man on New Hall Lane offered to show me his books and sell me his business. His turnover was £300, but he quietly told me about another £300 a week recorded in another book that the tax man knew nothing about. Obviously I was not interested.

At the end of my working day, Anne used to come to meet me at the railway station or off the bus at Bay Horse. I remember her dressed in her brown wool two-piece suit with cream edging, pushing the huge Silver Cross pram containing Timothy. We'd often walked this road when we were courting, when I went to meet Anne off the bus after her work. It was two and a half miles from

Dolphinholme to Bay Horse, but no problem to me back then. I always 'acted brave' walking back with Anne through the subway under the railway and the woods, yet on my way there I'd run like mad through the woods at Foxholes and under the subway because I was frightened to death of the unknown.

Kraft used to tell us, 'We don't want order-takers, we want salesmen. Make todays objection a sharpener to make tomorrow's sales talk sharper.' They meant that when we'd finished selling we should be so good that the customer would buy without objection. If someone objected to a sale then I hadn't done my job properly. Kraft showed us a picture of a balloon representing all the possible objections, which deflated as the customer talked until there were no more objections. Then we had to start selling. If we had something special to sell, we kept it in our pocket or bag until we had got our order, then produced this gem to be an extra, not part of the regular sale. I got orders just from being friendly and I realised I was an order-taker and not a salesman.

I did some relief work for a salesman traveller in Blackpool who accompanied me to help with the first few shops. His opening words to each shopkeeper were, 'Good morning. What have you had from Kraft through the wholesaler this week?' He'd write their reply down as if it were an order, then destroy the copy for the wholesaler so it looked as if he'd sold it himself. Eventually Kraft began to do direct selling. They built a factory at Liverpool. I said to the Kraft bosses, 'You are putting your factory in the wrong place because the Liverpool folk are always striking.'

Nevertheless, Kraft built their factory in a deprived area of Liverpool. Later when we had haulage wagons I was scared to death of the union people on the docks, because one wrong word or action from us or anyone could cause them to come out on strike. We needed three or four men to empty or load containers, but eventually only two men working each container was sufficient. On the docks they had sixteen men, working in groups of eight on alternate days, yet they all got paid full-time. A lad who worked for his uncle took coffee beans from the docks to York. One day the uncle got reprimanded because his nephew was helping the men to load the beans. He was not allowed to help, but just had to just watch.

Mr Bee, the local dairyman and a trustee at the church, offered me a job selling cheese, but I wasn't a salesman. He was going to pay me 11 pounds per week but my dad offered me the same money to work at home. And so it was I came back to work for him.

Dolphinholme – The Centre of Our World

Dolphinholme was a mill village. I always thought that the two rows we lived on had been built by the mill owners benevolently for their workers to inhabit, but then I read a history of Dolphinholme by David Ollerton (a dissertation completed for his teacher training) and discovered they'd been constructed as two-up two-downs with the main room containing a weaving loom in which tenants had to work, weaving wool products for the mill owners who sold them on. The goods were taken from the village through

Lower Dolphinholme and up the Wagon Road on the way to Yorkshire.

The toilets and coal-houses were situated between the two terraces. The toilets were emptied once a month by a man called Teddy Kec, who had a horse and cart. He wheelbarrowed the contents of thirty-six toilets down to the end of the alley and then, right opposite our back door, he'd load this dreadful stuff into his cart. The stench was terrible. At lunch-time Teddy Kec would happily sit beside his cart and munch on his sandwiches. Our own toilet was approximately fifty metres from our house so if anyone had a stomach upset in the night – it doesn't bear thinking about. I can say that our toilet lid was quite modern having two holes, a large one and a smaller one to prevent the children falling through into the pit below!

Dolphinholme Village was great what with the camaraderie and everyone knowing everybody else's business. Yes, it was a wonderful place to live. We were only three hundred metres from the Mill Wood and the River Wyre where, as children, we spent hours playing.

During the time that my parents ran the Dolphinholme Stores, Sunday night suppers were quite a thing in our home. It was often a full salad supper. Others would join us, such as the Rhodes family from Lower Moorhead Farm who had been to Dolphinholme Chapel that evening. My sister Betty and I remembered their eldest son James would sit at the table; he'd not say, 'Please can you pass the bread?' but demanded in a deep voice, 'Bread. Bread!'

Our Shop and the Midnight Grocer

Singletons had previously owned the shop but they'd gone bankrupt. My dad, Harold, was a fully qualified grocer serving his apprenticeship at TD Smiths in Lancaster (who at that time were on a par with WH Booths in Preston). Also for a short time, Dad worked at a shop in Liverpool as part of his apprenticeship for TD Smiths. When the opportunity rose to buy the shop in Dolphinholme, to his credit he borrowed some money and got the business re-ignited and developed it successfully, eventually handing it on to me. Dad made me aware that even though Peter at that time was working in the bank, and Betty was working part-time in the shop (when she was well enough) they were to have equal shares in the whole business.

These men worked with Dad (Harold) before I took over the shop.
Dad had the big windows put in. Left: Charlie Singleton (Chuck).
Right: Brian Dodding. Centre: Sorry, I can't remember!

The shop was Dad's life. He was very happy simply letting it tick over. He was known as "the Midnight Grocer," not because he worked his socks off for long hours, but because of his erratic time-keeping, he'd often end up delivering groceries late into the evening. (Most likely, he'd have been playing draughts with Jack Kidd on his way home from delivering orders around Catshaw).

For me, running the shop was fine. The only arguments I had with my father concerned him not finishing work on time. Before Anne and I moved to the shop, Dad would rise at 7am to let in the bread-man then he'd eat breakfast, read the paper, have a shave, and not appear back in the shop until after 9am. When I began working in the shop we agreed to close for lunch from 12.30 until 1.30pm, during which Dad took a nap and woe betide anyone who woke him before 2pm that afternoon! Afterwards we would be delivering to the farms at all hours.

Dad would go into Lancaster to Ben Riley's for wholesale groceries. On his return, we'd unload and sort it out. We'd write down a 'bit list' of things to ensure we had everything to fulfil customer orders. When the stuff came in we'd divide it into the order boxes before heading for the hills, but we couldn't actually do the bit list until Dad returned from Lancaster. He'd be gone from 11am but not land back until well after 2pm. What had he been up to? Most likely camping (*chatting*) with Ben Riley who incidentally had been his best man at his wedding. I then suggested to Dad that instead of him going every Tuesday and Friday to pick up the groceries from Lancaster, Riley's should be delivering them to us because we were good customers, paying Rileys two or three hundred pounds per week. Our other wholesalers, G&W Collins and Palmer and Harvey's both from Preston, already delivered to us directly.

I always wanted to finish work as soon as possible because with Anne's help I then had time to do other business, such as driving for other folk to make more money. So when I was in charge of things, I'd be able to make extra money picking chickens up during the night.

As a three-year old child at Portree, Timothy had constantly claimed that one day he'd go to school from the shop, even though we had never even discussed moving there. But Timothy's pronouncement came true and he *did* go to school from the shop. A year or two after Timothy's 'prophetic' word, before Dad finally retired, we exchanged homes – my parents and Betty moved to Portree, while Anne, myself, Timothy and Andrew moved to the shop.

New housing was being developed around Dolphinholme. Church Close was built, along with four agricultural cottages opposite the shop. (We used to sail little boats in the water in the footings of these buildings, it was that wet, but once they'd laid floorboards over it all, you couldn't see the water!) Brookfield Close was constructed below Portree. And still the council had further plans for development. This increase in the local population gave me the idea that we should modernise the shop and go semi-self-service. I suggested this to Dad, because I'd seen how this method had worked in the Preston shops when I was selling Kraft. To my father's credit he agreed and said, 'I'll sell the Stable Yard and use the money for our redevelopment.' Considering Dad could be a bit of a stick-in-the-mud I admired him for being so forward-thinking. Then I thought it would be a very good thing if I could buy the Stable Yard from Dad.

So I approached Uncle William, who owned five farms in the Cotswolds, to ask if he would lend me some money to purchase the Stable Yard. Uncle William was my mother (Gwen's) brother. He married Aunty Lilian who was a somewhat hoity-toity woman. She watched the pennies carefully. We'd see her removing the mould from jam before she put the jam on the table and considered this to be very posh! William and Lilian had moved down south so William could manage farms for the landed gentry. When my other uncles saw his progress they all moved south too! (Except for Uncle George and Aunty Peg Kelsall who farmed at Colne, East Lancs.) Work-wise they were successful, soon owning their own farms, except for Uncle George and Aunty Mary Townley who was my mother's sister. George tried farming but he had little business acumen. He therefore worked for his brother-in-laws, Uncle David and Uncle Joe, who had started farming together at Syde and Harcombe.

Anyway, Uncle William was so miserable that he refused to lend me the £500. Later I learnt that cousin Aubrey Townley had also asked William for money and he wouldn't lend him any either. All the same, Aubrey did financially well with his milk-round and his hens. In the end I borrowed the money from the bank and bought Stable Yard off Dad and he then was able to use this money to modernise the shop. I decided the shop should become a 'VG' (similar to Spar) because I'd seen G.W. COLLINS of Corporation Street, Preston - a VG that competed with the larger supermarkets with their special offers. Business people from VG came to help us arrange the shop, and Heinz, Hartleys and other firms helped fill the shelves with their own products. Eventually the only thing we served to our customers was bacon, ham and cheese. We used the slicer for everything and only cleaned it fortnightly. We cut cooked ham on the same machine as the raw bacon. Everyone was getting immunised! The new shop floor was no longer caked in sultanas and sugar and stuff, forcing us to stop and scrape it clean.

Whilst we were modernising the shop we were also altering the house. The house and the shop were one building, but not fit for purpose. The layout was poor. We kept stock in a cellar which was liable to flood, so I purchased an old small fridge store for bacon, ham and other perishables. The main warehouse was another cottage on the terrace but it was at the back of our home. (In effect, we owned two of the cottages and the shop premises). When we were putting the orders up, and they were complete, we'd then pack them into a box and carry them through our kitchen and lounge, where a long mat was laid to protect the carpet. My mother once said, 'If anyone falls ill, collapse on this mat, because then you'll be in the way and someone will have to pick you up.' Not only did we carry the orders through our lounge, we also had to go through it to the back to collect stock for the shop shelves. We solved the problem by converting the large upstairs storeroom into a lounge with steps up the outside of the house to give us access. Then we blocked off the indoor stairs that led from the shop.

*

There were heavy wooden beams crossing the roof that the joiner told us could be removed. One of the huge beams was set into the chimney wall of the house. When we removed this, we discovered that over half a metre had been badly charred and blackened as if it had threatened to catch fire. We'd been very fortunate. For years, to clean the chimney Dad would put a sack soaked in paraffin oil on the fire, and then hold a blower over the fire. The blower was a piece of sheet tin for drawing the fire, about 2 feet square with a handle attached. This would glow red hot, then it drew the air underneath the grate and the fire would go up the chimney. The soot would catch fire, covering the village in black smoke for about twenty minutes. No wonder that beam was black and burnt! In any case, the beam shouldn't have been in the chimney - it could have burnt through into the house. I suspect the reason no fire had taken hold was that there hadn't been sufficient oxygen in the chimney.

Another Fire Story

Doreen Cookson worked for us in the shop part-time. She lived on the front row at Dolphinholme. Her chimney was sooted up and it ignited. The fire brigade arrived and poured water down the chimney to extinguish it. The whole village turned out to watch this exciting event. How Doreen dealt with the water in the fireplace I've no idea.

Profits and Pigs

We were delivering bread twice a week to farms in the area as far as Tarnbrook. Believe it or not the postman had been doing this for the princely sum of a fiver at Christmas! Postmen used to deliver a variety of things for people and were very helpful. It started with the postman delivering barm yeast so people could use it to make bread, but when sliced bread came in we changed to giving the postman two trays of bread for our list of customers. When postmen were no longer allowed to do this, my dad took on this work. About this time, I discovered that many farmers were beginning to buy flour and tea in bulk from their cattle-food providers. Also, the new supermarkets began to sell all sorts to locals. I knew I had to compete with them.

One day, I sat down and analysed the cost of putting the orders up and delivering groceries to the outlying farms and realised we were only making £5 profit a day. It wasn't worth the effort. I decided to stop all deliveries, except for the Quernmore round which was always profitable. Anne and a girl could run the shop and post-office (the post-office offered a reasonable income) and I'd find something else to do. By this time we had three children, Timothy, Andrew and Cherith. Combining parenting with shop work didn't faze Anne one bit.

A big new estate was being developed at Pleckgate, Blackburn. Part of this plan included a creating a new superstore for VG and I'd agreed with VG that I would open this. I arranged to borrow £4000 from the bank and £4000 from John Bee to open it. While running the Dolphinholme VG, I earned extra money by driving part-time for Ronald Kenyon who had two cattle trucks. I used to go up to Cavaghan and Gray at Carlisle to drop a load of pigs off for slaughter. Occasionally, Anne came with me for company leaving the girls in the shop to watch the children.

I also drove for a rather lazy man called Colin Parker who owned two trucks in which he picked up chickens for the factory at Green Lane in Garstang. My job was to drive one of these trucks to fetch the chickens from the broiler farms. I would arrive home at 3 - 4am. It was quite a job because we had to pick the empty crates from the front of the lorry to start the loading process and these would be stacked 7 or 8 crates high. The wagon used to be weighed out and then in. We had to check that no farmer had put stones inside the spare wheel to be weighed in as chickens! We sometimes drove as far as Cannock, near Birmingham. One bank holiday we went to collect new young hens at the point of lay, (pullets), from the south coast to Pilling. It took a full twenty-four hours. That was some job.

I mentioned that I'd stopped delivering groceries around the farms. Immediately after I stopped this unprofitable work, Ronald Kenyon had a serious accident with his cattle truck. The gates for loading the cattle were on the outside of the ramp of his wagon instead of inside. (If they were on the inside, you closed the gates in, which fastened the cattle in, *then* put the tailgate up.) As Ronald was putting up the tailgate, a cow jumped against it and seriously crushed him beneath the tailgate. The result was that I ran Ronald's business for the next two months while he recuperated. I had a battle to get eight shillings per hour out of Ronald because while I was working for him I had to pay a girl to cover my duties in the shop.

My work for Ronald included taking his cattle to auction in Lancaster and other jobs he usually did for farmers, including taking rolled-up wool from sheep clippings through to Bradford. One of these loads slipped to one side and I drove all the way to Bradford sitting on the right cheek of my bottom, trying to keep the wagon straight! When I stopped at traffic lights, people knocked on my wagon door to ask, 'Do you know your load has slipped?' Did I?! The relief on reaching Bradford without everything falling off was tremendous. I'm sure my efforts of *leaning-to-one-side* definitely helped.

At the auction mart I met Tom Holmes who'd had a heart attack and could no longer continue with his coach-driving business. His brother had owned W.H. Holmes Transport Ltd which had nine cattle trucks at Brock. When his brother died suddenly, Tom bought W.H. Holmes Transport Ltd. I'd met Tom before, when he drove coaches because each year on Whit-Monday he'd drive thirty of us from Dolphinholme to an event at Cliff College, Calver, near Sheffield. We'd take sandwiches and drinks. One year, the famous evangelist Billy Graham was there. It was pouring with rain. I remember that the whole hour as Billy spoke, the rain stopped. I remember that Pastor Barrie and Eva Walton were also present.

Anyway, I met Tom Holmes and told him what I was doing with the bank and how I was going to open the VG shop in Blackburn. Tom told me that his own business was for sale and it would cost about the same amount as we were about to pay for Pleckgate. (We considered buying it, but Tom had 'failed' to inform us that his sister-in-law Dora had a £5000 debenture in the company which would need paying off in a few years' time). The cost of my house had been £2000, which offers a comparison to the £8000 price of the business. I thought and prayed about the matter and went to see my brother Peter who worked in Bolton for Nat West bank. I asked Peter if he wanted to come into business with me. He agreed and arrangements were made. On our way to finalise things, Peter and I stopped the car in Catterall and prayed about what we were going to do. Then we went to see Tom Holmes. We bought WH Holmes Transport Ltd on that very day in 1969. We felt it was God-opportune because in the end the development with the new VG at Pleckgate didn't open for eighteen months. Anne would always agree with whatever I was doing. I would talk to her about things and she'd just say 'Yes.'

We got the money despite the nation being pressurised by a labour credit squeeze. I'd intended to get half from the bank but suddenly they wouldn't lend me a thing, so Peter and I visited John Bee of Bee's Dairy at Haverhill to ask him to lend us *all* the money and he agreed. John had a big heart; we were not the first people he'd helped start up in business. So Peter ran the shop and I began working with the haulage. I stayed for two weeks with Tom and his wife to learn the ropes of the business.

Towards the end of the fortnight Tom dropped a bombshell, saying, 'Now, you'll be able to run the business from Stable Yard at Dolphinholme because this house and land is mine. It doesn't belong to W.H. Holmes Transport.' We had been naïve and had never questioned that the house and land had not been included in the sale. Peter and I were forced to get a mortgage to purchase the Hollies at Joe Lane, Catterall.

We took over the licenses for running wagons. In those days you ran on A, B and C licenses; each one restricted you to a certain thing such as a cattle truck or a flat truck. It was not possible to change a contract part-way, for example, a license could not be changed from a cattle truck to a flat truck without permission from the licensing authority and this could be challenging because on the licensing board were British Road Services, a nationalised industry, and British Railways. They were always objecting to us trying to do different things with our vehicles.

Peter's children, Philip and Katie, had been born in Bradford. The family were transferred by Nat West from Bradford to live in Bolton. They then moved to live with Dad and Mum for a while (1969). After Peter and I purchased the Hollies, Peter lived there for a while. I lived in the shop but I had to go down to work at Catterall while Peter came up to run the shop at Dolphinholme. He was financially good with all the businesses, having been an accountant for eighteen months and working in the bank for seven years. Peter said, 'Money is like a commodity on a shelf. You use it as you want to.' Our families eventually swapped houses, as the present situation was ridiculous.

In the middle of all this, we had to collect Tom Holmes debts for W.H. Holmes Transport. Farmers were notoriously slow at paying their bills. After six months our accountant said, 'If Tom Holmes doesn't leave his money with you for another year you are going to be in trouble, because you are under-capitalised. You will be finished.' So Peter and I set off to Tom Holme's house in Torquay in a second hand MG 1100 twin carbs, because the new Wolsley I'd bought on hire purchase whilst working at the shop (when I was on £35 per week minus bills) was no longer affordable. We asked Tom Holmes if he would leave his debts in for another eighteen months or two years. If he hadn't agreed, we'd have had to return and declare ourselves voluntarily bankrupt. He was guarding his own interests because if there had been a shortfall he would have suffered – he needed us NOT to go bankrupt so he didn't lose out. The accountant also made us increase our charges by 10%.

The shop had been my life until ASDA opened and took our customers. I sympathise with modern small shops because this is what happened to us. When Asda started they were discount stores. When you went to ASDA, the Brooke Bond rep and other reps were keeping ASDA's shelves full of tea or whatever product they sold. We could not compete pricewise so became a convenience store.

The Beginning of Things Coming to Us

Dad said to me, 'You are never happy unless you are doing something new.' He'd notice and remark at how happy I was taking on any new project. New things did come to us; opportunities were always fruitful. To this day, I still enjoy fresh perspective and motivation.

*

A man called Harry Bland rang up out of the blue and said, 'Why don't you lads take over this place?' I asked, 'Why us?' because we knew another haulier named Jack Chippendale who'd done a lot of work for Harry. At first we declared, 'We can't afford to buy it.' Harry ran a business from The Old Threshing Yard on Hollins Lane which is now called Thresher's Court. Harry stored fertiliser for ICI and he had two tipper wagons for carting ash from Fleetwood ICI works to Billingham during the night and then he'd return with fertiliser for the store in Hollins Lane. He was working nights and employed two men who worked days, so it was likely he was working himself to death and drinking at the same time. He was ready for out. Harry said, 'I'll rent the premises to you for £30 a week and the business goes with it. I have two tipper lorries but not enough work for them. You'll need to buy those from me.'

This we did. We kept one wagon as a tipper and converted one into a cattle truck. Harry told us the depot would hold 800 tons of fertiliser. We were paid by the tonnage in store then, and not for handling, but we managed to stack 1100 tons that winter.

Because we were moving business we sold the shop and post-office at Dolphinholme. Peter was going to run the ICI depot with Timothy which meant him moving house. Peter bought 'Colinfield' in Catterall. Aged 16, Tim left school. Every day he cycled to Forton to Thresher's Court. (This was the old yard where a man named Johnny Ball kept steam-engines and threshers for harvest-time as well as steam-rollers for road-rolling). Here, farmers came in to collect the fertiliser that they'd ordered through the cattle-food suppliers. Our wagons were bringing in fertiliser. By this time the ash business from Fleetwood had dried up so we sent wagons to collect fertiliser as necessary. We didn't realise it at the time, but we were coming in on the rising tide of fertiliser. We did such a good job handling the fertiliser and doing deliveries for some of the cattle food people that Preston Farmer's Ltd asked us to store fertiliser for them, which is why we rented the premises at Brock Auction. We stored over 1,000 tons of fertiliser at Brock.

One day at the auction I met a man called Geoffrey Bell who had a cattle truck business run from Thurnham. The solicitor who ran the property at Thurnham wanted Geoff Bell out because he didn't keep the premises tidy. Geoffrey had been looking at Greens Farm and offered Stewart Simpson the farmer £17,500 for 5 acres of Greens Farm at Winmarleigh plus a house and buildings but the farmer Stuart Simpson from Newhall Farm who also owned Greens Farm, wanted more. Peter and I asked Geoffrey if we went in with him and offered Stuart more, would Geoffrey agree for Peter and me to have an acre of land

and the Dutch Barn. Geoffrey agreed but he said it would be better if Stuart added a paddock at the bottom. So Peter and I went to see Stuart Simpson and asked him if he would add this little paddock at the bottom onto the deal and we would pay him 21 and a half thousand pounds. And he agreed. We purchased Greens Farm for £21,500. We kept the acre and Dutch barn and sold Geoffrey the rest for £17,500. It was good for all of us. We situated a small caravan on site for an office. The toilets were the nearest tree in the nearby wood. We added a lean-to onto the Dutch barn. We asked ICI if they would store with us there instead of at Hollins Lane. They agreed. They asked us to erect two more buildings at Greens Farm. We planted many trees around our boundaries because we wanted the place to look attractive. Because of expansion I moved a number of these trees three times. The Courier newspaper people from Garstang showed an interest in our Winmarleigh development. They took a photograph of one of our fork truck drivers, Clifford Trickett and myself planting the trees - well, pretending to! Just for the photo, I had posed with a shovel in my hand. One day a farmer came in for fertiliser. He'd seen the picture in the papers and said, 'Do you always plant trees with a size-ten shovel?' Part of Geoffrey Bell's land was across the other side of our buildings and yard. His land could be useful to us, so we asked, 'If we get you one and a half acres on the other side of your house, could we have the land adjacent to our land?' Stuart wanted to charge us £5,500. We said it was dear, but he assured us, 'It will seem like peanuts to you lads in a few years' time.' He asked his wife about the deal and she, 'Yes, but I want a Rover car if you do it!'

We built a lorry park on that land and we also erected a wagon-wash. At that time industrial land cost £40,000 an acre but we had only paid £5,500 for it. It turned out to be an excellent deal as Stuart had predicted.

We had applied to put up yet another building. The

My nephew Philip at Greens Farm

council were resisting our request, but we appealed and they agreed to visit us to look at the site. The planners arrived in a coach. We proudly showed off our pond full of lilies and all the trees and beautiful planting and they said, 'Yes, we will give you planning permission on the grounds that you never ask for another building to go on the site.' My brother Peter said, '*Never* is a long time.' We were delighted with the council response: I don't think they fully realised what they were giving us! We had two acres of parking area and a new ten-thousand square foot building.

Cattle Carting Continued

We used to collect Irish cattle at Birkenhead to take them to auction, mainly to York auction mart under the walls of York. Then one day Harold Baines took a load of Irish cattle in a Scania double-decker cattle truck to Banbury Auction and dropped his cattle off. It was 11.30pm when Harold phoned me to say, 'A man wants a load of cattle taking to Dover. Shall we do it?' (Our drivers were earning £15 a week back then). I told Harold it was up to him what he did and Harold said, 'He's given me a tenner. The jobs on!' The man gave him a cheque before he set off. This man's name was Dougie Clay.

We travelled all over Lancashire picking up calves to take to Sellet Mill near Kirkby Lonsdale where they were sorted out by the Lancashire Calf Club people for different customers as far away as Fife and even Aberdeen. Those days were long and hard - often we wouldn't be setting off from Sellet Mill for Scotland until two in the afternoon. One day, Victor Wells' wagon full of calves broke down on the way to Scotland and I had to set off with a relief wagon to deliver them with him, all the way up to Aberdeen. We hadn't had a drink as we arrived at the last farm at eleven o'clock that night. Victor and I were desperate for a drink. The farmer's wife enquired, 'Where have you come from?' 'Lancashire,' we replied, hoping to be offered a cup of tea. She said, 'Oh,' and 'Goodnight!'

We went to work for a man who had worked for Lancashire Calf Club but had since started his own business. We were moving calves for him and then, with our double-decker we were picking cattle up at Edinburgh Gorgie Cattle market and then bringing them to Gisburn auction for sale. We were owed money by this man. Peter and I went to see him one Friday night to collect a cheque for £1400. He said, 'If you take this cheque now, I am finishing with you.' We insisted on taking the cheque and by the following Tuesday he had phoned us to work for him again. We were checking with Nat West Bank in Kirkby Lonsdale for the next few weeks and they assured us all cheques were being honoured, but soon the man went broke. He owed us £1000. What we hadn't realised was that this man was buying cattle in Edinburgh and selling them at Gisburn Auction Mart to try to make a profit. He failed. He went to jail. The headline in the Lancaster Guardian ran, 'Rustler goes to jail for eighteen months.'

So then I contacted the aforementioned Mr Dougie Clay. I asked him, 'Can you use us as we have a double-decker cattle wagon but not enough work to do.' Mr Clay immediately said, 'Send your wagon to Banbury tomorrow.' So our driver Harold Baines drove the wagon there and worked all week for Mr Clay, carting cast cows (cows that have finished their milk production). Harold worked out of Banbury, Leicester, Chippenham and Derby. Every weekend Mr Clay gave him a blank cheque for me to fill in and telephone him on the Saturday to tell him what I had made it out for. Better still, for Harold, he also received a ten pound note in his hand – and that was on top of the fifteen pounds he was paid by us.

When my cousin Malcolm Whitaker knew we were working for Mr Clay he warned us that Clay was not a good man. A local haulier had given up all his other business to work for Mr Clay and after a while, they fell out over rates of pay. Mr Clay stopped him working, leaving the man without any business at all. Mr Clay wanted us to lay another wagon on – a double-decker. We said we couldn't afford to buy any more vehicles. He said, 'Buy it and I will pay, you pay me off as you use it.' Also he wanted one more wagon, so as we worked for him we ended up owning three double-deckers. The work with Mr Clay ended when a haulier from Alnwick area offered to work for him more cheaply. (Sheep on the cheap!) I was glad to finish because by this stage every time the phone went I was jumping. Mr Clay always pushed and pushed with no sympathy for our long hours. He was a hard task master.

On Mr Clay's first job cattle-dealing, he drove a very small van to a farm to buy a cow. The farmer said, 'If you can get that cow into that van you can have it.' And so Mr Clay did just that. He grabbed the nose of the cow and

shoved it over into the van and drove from the Midlands to the local abattoir with one hand clutching the nose of the cow and with the other he steered and changed gears!

Mr Clay used to buy 72 cows in Derby on a Saturday. He asked us to go on a Sunday to take them to Richmond-on-Thames abattoir but we told him, 'We don't work on a Sunday.' Mr Clay replied, 'I want them at the abattoir by 6am on Monday morning.' So our lads set off at 10pm on Sunday night to do his work. The next time I rang the auctioneer to line up the cattle at Derby on a Sunday he agreed, but it was so late at night he said he wouldn't do it again. I told Mr Clay what the auctioneer had said and Mr Clay replied, 'Mr Gardner, do it respectfully, but tell the auctioneer that if he isn't prepared to do it, Mr Clay can buy his cows elsewhere.' When I told the auctioneer what Mr Clay had said, he replied, 'I didn't know you were doing it for Mr Clay, I thought you were doing it for your own convenience.' I said, 'What? At one o'clock in the morning?' There was no problem after that.

Mr Clay was that sharp he could tell which wagon the cattle had been bought down in because of the marks on their bodies. Mr Clay always knew how far to push and then back off. He could say, 'I can afford to run my own haulage but I don't want the hassle, which is why I employ you so *you* have the hassle.'

At 4am, Tommy Graham went to pick cattle up in Stoke for Mr Clay. Anne and I were woken by a phone call asking where our driver was. I said, 'He is a new man and may be lost. There aren't many people about so early in the morning to ask directions from.' (No SAT NAV in those days!) Mr Clay said, 'I have people up at 4am to load him, so if he hasn't arrived by 4.30am I will ring you back again, Mr Gardner.' He never rang because thankfully Tommy made it in time.

We had bought a new MAN by this time. Tommy Graham was driving the MAN with a load of cattle for Mr

Clay, heading for London, but by Watford Gap he lost two wheels from the unit. (On a newly painted wheel the paint affects the wheels and you have to check them or they work loose.) I rang Mr Clay to explain, but gained no sympathy from him. 'You'll have to put another unit in won't you, Mr Gardner.' Our mechanic Geoff and I went to Watford with a spare unit. Tommy was then able to drive on while Geoff and I went into London MAN for parts and mended the unit by the roadside and brought it home.

The Men

We couldn't have succeeded without a solid team of men who loaded, drove, fettled, and added colour to our daily lives. Stephen Backhouse had a stammer, Jimmy Miller had a tick and Jack Moon (we called Shiner) was crippled. They had a great sense of humour – unless they were simply being naïve? I remember Shiner pointing up at the sky saying, 'See that jet up there? It followed me out Preston!'

While Anne's mother lived with us for ten years we were very short of money. One Saturday Anne and I had a row. To calm down I suggested a car ride to Hurst Green. We decided to eat at The Craven Heifer. We looked at the menu and chose a meal costing 25 shillings which was all we had on us. We ate, but we didn't really enjoy it. Then the bill came to 27 shillings and sixpence because they added service charges! I apologised that we didn't have another penny. The landlady said, 'It's all right.' But I said, 'We will have a wagon passing next Thursday.' The following Thursday, Jack Moon (Shiner) was returning from

Gisburn auction. He limped into the pub to drop off the half-crown we owed.

When Jack joined our firm we provided a special wagon for him that was legally within the weight so he could drive for us without having to pass his HGV test. Concerning Jack, a policeman in civvies approached me. He said, 'Your man has just backed into me at the auction mart. In fact, Jack had backed into him twice. The policeman said, 'It's all very well you being kind to your man, but if he hits and kills someone you will regret it.' Jack had a medical test and learnt that he had muscular dystrophy, but we had no idea how this affected him because he'd been so quick to fetch and load the cattle. Much later we discovered that the farmers had been doing all the work for him! Things came to a head when Shiner took cattle to Clarkson's abattoir in Preston. He'd backed in and hit their gutters. Clarkson's phoned us saying, 'Don't send that cripple into our yard again.'

Our mechanic Geoffrey knew everything about engines. He was untidy. He'd come to work carrying his tools in a sack. These would end up scattered all over the garage, but he'd know exactly what was what and where to find it. Geoff was a fettler, meaning he could dismantle and mend and weld things. He was brought up in the school of 'make-do-and-mend.' He was great. He used to say, 'Reet, I'm going home to fried lettuce.' His wife was also illiterate. Peter gave Geoff a wage rise to help him meet his mortgage, but there was no acknowledgement or thanks. Geoffrey never said thank you for anything - except for once. This was when we sold the company. I took him a £500 gift and he said, 'Thanks. I am going to get a new TV with this.' We needed two mechanics and our son David trained as one. He and Geoff worked together well. Geoffrey often showed him how to fettle instead of getting a new part.

Alnwick in Northumberland

The farmer hauliers from Kettering, (from the same farm we'd deliver lambs and reload on the way to Dover), were also working for Mr Clay. They had broken down at Alnwick and rang me to ask for help. I said, 'Sorry, we have no vehicle to help you,' but half an hour later, Mr Clay rang me about this. I replied, 'They are the hauliers, Mr Clay, and it is their responsibility, not ours.' At that time, my son Timothy had just returned from a run with Jimmy Miller (Tim was running on L-plates). Mr Clay said, 'Mr Gardner, those are my lambs on that wagon and I need them down to Dover.' Illegally, we sent Tim who was learning to drive an HGV and Jimmy Miller as the main driver, to Northumberland to pick up the lambs, which they did. By the time they arrived in Kent, they were so tired they drew onto a layby. Jim had been sleeping in the bunk when Tim was driving and vice versa. The police stopped to check them because they were parked up, and of course discovered what they'd been doing. We were up for twenty separate counts; driving without attention, driving all these miles without stopping, learner driver, main driver asleep and so on.

Mr Clay asked me if his solicitor should handle it and we said, 'Yes' and left it to them. They got many of the charges dropped and eventually, because a new EU ruling had just come out, that all animals had to arrive at their destination for food and water within twenty-four hours whatever the circumstances, we got off without a charge. So we got off lightly. Mr Clay's solicitor did us proud. We could have been done for thousands in fines but it cost us only £300 for the solicitor.

We were moving 500 lambs at a time from the Gorgie Markets in Edinburgh for Mr Clay. He was buying up to 2,000 lambs per week. We used to pick up 500 lambs each time and on our way south to Kettering, we'd stop at Catterall and load up with diesel at the Hollies. Anne was always distressed to see these lambs on the wagons, heading for slaughter. We would then proceed to Kettering, to the farm where we would unload, then move up three bays, then reload what we thought were fresh lambs onto our lorry. We'd proceed to Dover with them.

One day, two CID officers came in to our office at Hollies, and asked us if we were taking lambs for Mr Clay and we said yes. They said they would ignore anything illegal on hours and the tachographs if there *was* anything, so long as they could check our books and logs to check on Mr Clay, because he was shipping lambs to France and getting subsidy on them when they should have stayed for 29 days on a farm after being purchased in auction before moving on. I went to Kettering court. The judge asked me

Excerpts from two of a series of letters between Mr A.M. Burstow, 39, Queens Square, Crawley, Sussex, solicitors acting for Timothy Gardner and Mr Jimmy Miller at the 'HEARING at BATTLE' and David Gardner Snr for W.H. Holmes Transport Ltd c/o The Hollies, Catterall.

28th January 1977

Dear Mr Burstow,

Many thanks for your letter and excellent news that you agree to defend us. We do appreciate what you are doing on our behalf. Your assumption is correct. Would you please conduct this case for us and plead as you see fit. Timothy Gardner had only omitted to put in a meal break, which in fact they had had, your side of London.

Yours sincerely

David Gardner W.H. Holmes (Transport) Ltd

PS. If you ever decide to move North to the County of Counties - let us know!!!

From Mr Burstow, 18th February 1977

Dear Mr Gardner,

I am pleased to tell you that the result of the Hearing at Battle yesterday was very satisfactory. The bench were very sympathetic and agreed with me that on the question of priorities it was more important to get proper help and assistance to the sheep at the time than to worry too much about the records. Accordingly, both drivers were given absolute discharge which means of course that they are not to be punished in any way for the offences committed.

Obviously, in future . . . where events occur which are likely to cause danger to the life or health of individuals or animals, the best procedure is to keep a careful record of the hours actually worked so that it does not appear that there is an attempt to hide the true situation. I am not sure whether I agree with your comment about the 'County of Counties' but nevertheless I would be pleased to help at any time if you felt that I could give any advice.

Yours sincerely

AM Burstow

our connection with Mr Clay. I told him how it had begun and how Mr Clay had bought us other cattle trucks with no contracts signed, deals made over the phone and we paid him off as we used them. Every week, Mr Clay would send a blank cheque up with Harold Baines and ring up Saturday night to ask me how much I had made it out for. He never cared what time he phoned. Later I learned that he often did a lot of business from his bed. I added that despite everything, Mr Clay had been nothing but good for us. The judge laughed, 'And you are here for the prosecution?'

A year later I found out that the whole case had been scrapped. Mr Clay was getting export subsidy; he was tagging the lambs, altering the veterinary certificates that proved the lambs had been kept on a farm for a month – but Mr Clay was getting a subsidy from the government and the case was dropped. He got away with a lot. And he always used cash in hand.

It was alleged that Mr Clay lost a wagon in Belgium because it had been impounded. They weighed the wagon with the carcasses on and discovered that Mr Clay was cheating by putting pig-iron under the floor. He was getting paid the extra ton of pig-iron. Mr Clay was buying 2000 lambs at a time at Edinburgh market. It was a big market. He would always get these lambs because he could afford to pay a high price for them. The ordinary butchers could not afford these lambs and so were suffering. I think they blew the whistle on his terrible practices. Mr Clay was very clever with man management. He recognised when he'd gone too far and crossed the line of pushiness. I almost got to the point of finishing with him when he backed off with his demands. Over-stretching his men in the abattoir at Kingston-on-Thames took them almost to the point of walking out, when in he walked, their boss, with beer and sandwiches for all. And his pockets were positively bulging because he always had bundles of cash because farmers paid him luck money. Luck money is when a farmer sells an animal he'll give the buyer anything from two to five pounds for luck. This made the dealers more inclined to purchase that farmer's cattle.

We finally finished working for Mr Clay when a haulier in the north-east began to cart his lambs more cheaply for him. I told Mr Clay we couldn't compete with that low price so I said we'd return the double-decker that we still owed him £800 for. He said, 'What am I going to do with it?' and we told him, 'You'll sell it easily enough,' which he did. It took me about six months to stop jumping with nerves every time the phone rang.

Cattle and My Modus Operandi

One of the best jobs we had, and the most interesting, was with British Livestock Company from Sawbridgeworth in Hertfordshire. A man called Dick Gladstone from Levens near Witherslack, who worked buying cattle for British Livestock Company, asked us if we could transport a load of Friesian heifers in calf from Scotland to Bishop's Stortford. We had to pick them up during the day, because the other man who worked for Mr Gladstone picked them up at all times, including the night, but the big Scottish farmers didn't like loading their cattle in the dark, after their men had gone home. I agreed to pick up the heifers in daytime and get them down to Bishop's Stortford asap. I said to Dick, 'Next time you get a list of cattle to collect, meet me at Lancaster auction.' This happened. Dick gave me a list of 67 cattle to go to Lowestoft docks, then onto Spain. I said to Dick, 'Give me that list, I'll see that job is done. I'll telephone the farmers to give them the expected time of collection. Also, I will get these cattle to Lowestoft in time for the boat.' Dick was glad to do this as not having to organise the haulage took a weight off his mind.

I would write *Modus Operandi* on top of the lists I'd written out for the lads, to collect the cattle. We had five or six wagons going into Scotland; we went to Fife, Montrose and Aberdeen. Our secretary Mrs McKenna used to say, 'Why do you write Modus Operandi on top of that list?' I'd thought it was obvious. I'd never learnt Latin, but to me, this meant 'Method of Operation!' Mrs McKenna was pedantic at work. Sometimes she would correct my speech. For example, I'd say 'Millinthorpe' and she would say, 'It's not Millinthorpe, it's MILNthorpe. There's no 'i' in Milnthorpe.' (I was only pronouncing the name the way my mother had done – Millinthorpe). Mrs McKenna may have been a pedant at work but her home was somewhat chaotic. You'd think she'd be equally fastidious wherever she was but she couldn't get on top of organising her home! She was great at taking orders and doing the books and things, working alongside Dora Holmes who was the wife of the 'WH' of W.H. Holmes Transport Ltd. Whenever any of the men had used the phone, Mrs McKenna would wipe it. The office in which she worked was no more than a hut with a section with a counter for the men to come into. The hut was situated just up the yard from our house. At night, Anne and I used to sneak into that office and smoke two Consulate cigarettes. We thought the kids wouldn't know, but of course they did. They found out all sorts of things that we never knew about for years!

We did a lot of work for the British Livestock Company, even taking their cattle for France to Plympton in Devon. We were picking up in-calf heifers from South Wales; Harold Baines with the double-decker, being fed by the smaller wagon, driven by Stephen Backhouse. Harold was based at Cardiff and Stephen was going out all over South Wales as far as Haverford West. Harold and Stephen rang one night at 11.30pm to say, 'We've got the cattle done.' I said, 'Oh, good, you'll be coming home now,' thinking they'd arrived at Ivybridge. Stephen said, 'I am coming back, but Harold is just setting off to go to Ivybridge. We have just finished loading in Cardiff. The next time you plan picking cattle up in South Wales, allow an extra three hours!'

Once when Anne and I were on holiday in Cornwall, our driver Tommy Graham was down at Ivybridge. We invited him for tea in the Caravette, which he was pleased about. Whenever we saw our wagons on the road, we were always chuffed to bits. Another time Peter and I had taken a large double-decker cattle truck to Ivybridge. We discovered a road leading back up to Exeter and we took it but as we travelled the road narrowed. It became narrower and narrower. We were worried we'd get stuck, but thankfully we made it.

One driver used to do terrible things, damaging his wagon if he didn't want to go somewhere. He once rang me from Gisburn on his way to Lowestoft, and said, 'The wagon has broken down.' It was one of the larger wagons which held more cattle. Peter and I had to go there in *two* wagons, off-load them, load up in Gisburn, take the cattle to Lowestoft and then turn around. We arrived at Lowestoft as the lads who were already there were preparing to return to Catterall. They helped Peter and I unload and we set off back with them - fourteen hours of non-stop driving! It turned out the wayward driver had deliberately put a bolt across the fuses in his wagon to short the electrics because he was too lazy to go to Lowestoft. Previously, this man had worked for Collinsons. They had given him a reasonable reference, but I found out that if they sent him somewhere in winter, he'd phone to say that snow was blocking the road, and just return. I had no choice but to sack the man. His fiancée and her mum came and pleaded with me to keep him on. I said, 'Sorry, but we have to be reliable in what we do.' The trouble was I knew them from Caldervale Methodist Chapel.

An announcement in the Personal column - the Times newspaper Saturday 31st 1993:
TO ALL AUTHENTIC SAFEGARD SPOTTERS – don't worry about the Eddie and Norbert fuss in the Sunday Times. You are a rarer breed. Call for a cup of coffee at our HQ only 350 yards from Junction 34 on M6. Peter Gardner. PS I will be hard to catch next week, getting ready for the Garstang Show 7th August.

Another time we had to take 500 Galloway cattle for British Livestock to go to Russia from Dumfries and Galloway. We collected them up into Brock auction (Brock auction were good at allowing us to use their premises for holding cattle). On the Saturday morning, we set off with eight lorries to Lowestoft to go by cargo boat to Russia. I filmed this adventure using a super eight film camera! I stood in the road at Brock filming as the lorries exited the auction mart. So exciting - and I still have that film.

We used to go to a Cryological centre near Whitehaven. (At this place they took viable foetuses out of quality animals and implanted them in those of poorer quality, in order to repeat the insemination process more often.) We picked up two cows worth £2-300 each, but they had been artificially inseminated by sperm from posh beasts that were worth a whole pile of money! The cows themselves had little value, but what was inside was worth thousands. To think we were transporting only *two* cows all the way down to Hertfordshire.

Crewe auction held a special Friesian sale every month on a Friday. We collected cattle from farms as far north as Kendal, down to Winstanley, Wigan. One farmer from north of Kendal always dosed his cattle for sale with a pint of paraffin. He claimed it made them look better! We drove down on the Thursday with two or three wagon loads, leaving two men and wagons down at Crewe for any 'returns' or cattle bought on the Friday. ('Returns' were cattle that had not reached the reserve price.) The men stayed over. Overnight, they'd earn extra by cleaning the cows ready for sale on the Friday, so all the farmer had to do was to appear and sell his cow. They were generally generous with our lads for doing this mucky job.

Mr Tom Jolly from Great Eccleston always sent his cows to Crewe, and never to the Lancaster Friesian sale. The Friesian world was very important in Lancashire; all the Friesian farmers knew each other and their precious cattle extremely well. These farmers were fussy about their wagons and how we handled them.

We used to take cattle to Harrogate for the Yorkshire show before they changed the rules saying the cattle had to arrive on a Sunday. Because it was the Sabbath we didn't want to do that. We considered getting some other hauliers to do it for us. In the end we decided this would be hypocritical of us, so Peter or myself took the cattle to Harrogate to the show on the Sunday after all.

Bamfords, the cattlefood producers, lived at Brockbottoms. They wanted some horses to go to the Good Friday race trials at Gisburn. Anne and I, with two of our children, transported their horses for them. We enjoyed watching the horse trials for several hours. It was at the top of the hill just outside Clitheroe, Chatburn. For us, it was a fine day out and we were paid too.

On Saturdays, we often took Irish cattle from Birkenhead to York auction. One day, Peter and I had a load to transport from Birkenhead to a field on the Hellifield Road. Peter's son, Joe and my son Simon were with us – the lads were only about 10 years-old. We ask them to stand up the road to stop the cattle passing them, to turn them into a field. As the cattle came towards them, the lads accidentally let some cattle pass them. The cattle ran further up the road into a field owned by Malcolm Skidmore, auctioneer and local preacher. We had to sort those cattle out from Malcolm's own cattle and get them back across the road. What a nightmare! Peter and I were not happy but, after all, the boys were only very young.

All this time we were increasingly involved in the world of fertiliser storage. My back was becoming more and more painful. The cattle job was beginning to dry up. For example, we had worked for Lancashire Friesian calf club, taking calves up into Scotland, and also for Bibby's and BOCM weaner pigs and stores, weekly. Now these trips were few and far between. On top of all this, Walls phoned me to ask us to pick up their pigs, which would have been a huge job. However, they wanted us to do this on a Sunday. We suggested that we could fetch them really early Monday morning, but Walls weren't happy about that. So I said, 'Try Gibsons.' They did, and Gibsons got the contract. Farmers were buying their own trailers for moving stock. We were gradually going over to more flat haulage, until eventually we sold up the remains of the cattle business.

W.H. Holmes Trading as Safegard Storage Celebrates 90 Years!

Local Guardian business page headlines 28th Oct 1994 Four celebrations in one for Safegard's top team.'

1) 25 years since June 16th 1969 when Peter and David Gardner purchased W.H. Holmes transport company

2) 10 years since they bought waste ground on Caton Road, Lancaster on which to build their thriving business

3) 20 years since they formed a business relationship with MAN trucks

4) 90 years since Mr T. Holmes formed the original transport business with horse-drawn carts and landaus carrying bricks and paper in Brock

The Guardian recorded the following statement:

'All Safegard Storage staff were treated to an open day celebration with a slap-up buffet. The MAN company honoured Safegard by bringing their display trucks to Lancaster, including some vintage vehicles. The Gardner brothers have turned this into a very successful enterprise which now occupies more than 35,000 square feet on the Lansil Industrial estate in Lancaster along with the Caton Road depot and another centre in Winmarleigh, near Garstang. The bulk of the business comes in the form of Scott paper products, such as Andrex toilet tissue, which are transported across England. The company also offers a repackaging service for Burtons Biscuits. Their relabelled packets head from the Lancaster warehouse to Europe. Their dedicated staff meet the most demanding deadlines. The letters GARD reflect the first four letters in the family name GARDNER, to create the logo SAFEGARD.

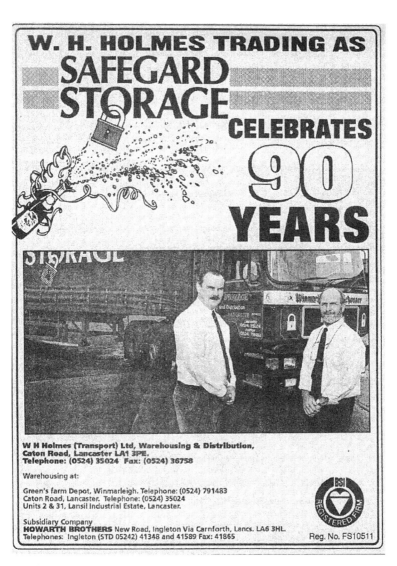

My son, David, with my brother Peter,
advertising Safegard in the local paper

From Cattle Haulage to Fertiliser Storage

Greens Farm was a springboard for everything that happened next. I did all the preparation in the yard at Greens Farm using Tom Pye's JCB. We had an artic tipper-trailer with a donkey engine on it - an engine attached to the trailer with the hydraulics for tipping.

Tom Pye was a farmer from New Hollies, a self-made man and a hard worker who had bought another farm at Cabus for £29,000. When the auctioneer said superciliously, 'Mr Pye, we require a deposit,' Tom replied, 'Tha'll at lot.' ('You'll get the lot – every penny – now.') Tom was a Free Mason. One day he approached me and asked if I'd do a job for him. He said, 'It's what friends are for.' What he was implying was that I'd borrowed his JCB and now it was my time to pay him back. He said, 'Would you level a car-park for me at Garstang? I need you to bring in some gravel with your tipper which I will pay for and you can level it out using my JCB.' So I levelled the Free Masons' car park, much to the amusement of the people at chapel. We had to put a new piston in the engine and a tyre on his JCB but it was well worth it because we used it often.

Bradshaw Brothers was a small haulier with premises for sale at Leck, Cowan Bridge. We looked and bought their place. We asked for planning permission to build a 1700 sq. foot unit but we were only allowed 1500 sq. feet because we weren't employing enough people. Mervyn France ran this unit for us, then Martin Gott who had previously worked for Kidds Haulage, took over. We hoped to borrow £16,000. The bank wanted all kinds of securities so Peter contacted a Preston friend from his Nat West days. The friend said, 'Send me your accounts.' He was so happy with Peter's accounts that he asked us how much money we needed. For that reason, we moved our business to the Nat West Bank.

We were storing fertiliser in five separate locations; Cowan Bridge, Caton Road in Lancaster, Glasson Dock, Greens Farm in Winmarleigh, and Burscough. We only had three or four accounts with cattle food firms and ICI. We realised we needed to diversify as we had virtually all our eggs in one basket.

Excerpt from Motor Transport Magazine August 23rd 1990

ICI FEAR – 80 fertiliser distributors around Teeside are anxiously waiting to hear whether ICI has been persuaded to keep its agricultural chemicals operations going. W.H. HOLMES (Transport) of Lancaster which trades as Safegard Storage, has five trailers with piggy-back fork trucks dedicated to the ICI fertilisers business. Manager David Gardner said, 'We have special short trailers, 26ft long which can deliver into the small Lancashire dairy farms. We receive bulk deliveries from ICI to store in our depots before making these deliveries.'

Safegard has just been awarded BS 5750 Part Two for transport and storage at all four of its depots. It has bases at Lancaster, Garstang, Burscough and Cowan Bridge. Mr Gardner added, 'ICI is one of our major customers. ICI plans to pass on its fertiliser business to Kamuri, a firm that supplies directly from its factory to the farm, so we will lose business as an intermediate storage and transport facility.'

We sold The Hollies, our family home with the premises and moved to a new house called Haverhill on Wham's Lane. Ironically, this house had once belonged to John and Irene Bee, the couple who originally lent us the money to start up in business, from what was then *their* front room. Circles. When we moved to Haverhill it was the first time the family hadn't lived directly aside the business. I soon enjoyed digging a huge fishpond that a surveyor later described as 'a shallow swimming pool in the garden.' In fact, before the fish were introduced Andrew and Katharine did swim in it. Andrew could dive in one end, do one stroke and touch the other side!

We hired a building of about 10,000 sq ft. on Caton Road. The man that rented out the building had already rented the next door structure to Edmund Metcalfe, who stored bone-meal in it, a by-product from his dead cattle processing business at Nightingale Hall. It stunk something awful! The owner wanted the bone-meal out. We told him *we* would rent it which got me into trouble with Edmund Metcalfe. He wrote to me saying I had done a wrong thing as a Christian brother! On reflection, he was right, we should not have pursued this. We looked at another building down at Heysham which was the right price, but it took Peter and I so long to travel there and back we decided it would waste too much time for lorries to cross to the motorway every day.

R. O. Hodgsons of Carnforth was buying a place on Caton Road in Lancaster. A man called Ron Walker worked for ROH as general manager. Ron said, 'We've got this great place on Caton Road. We plan to put a sign above it so everyone can see it from the M6. If you lads can get 30,000 square feet somewhere near, I will use you for overflow.' Pinkus commercial agents were looking for buildings for us. They came back with the site that Ron Walker had already told us Hodgsons were already buying.

Hodgsons was owned by China Clay, but Ron's manager was not cooperative with the manager of Courtaulds, who were selling half of their premises on Caton Road. Ron explained that his boss had tried to negotiate like a bull in a china shop. Courtauld's manager told me later that he had arranged an appointment with Ron's manager, and all he received was a note telling him what *he* wanted. Not the best way to do business!

Our connection with Ron

Ron Walker welcomed by Peter and myself

Ron's drinking buddy, Roy Adamson, had recently decided to become a Christian. Previously he'd been a nominal Roman Catholic but the apple of his eye, (his daughter,) was attending our youth group at Garstang Free Methodist Church and Roy came along check up to ensure we were not misleading her. Roy, being Roy, read all he could about what was so interesting to his daughter and soon he became a Christian. He then witnessed to his drinking buddy Ron and Ron's wife, Sylvia. Ron was a gentle giant of a man, who had played rugby for Salford and only retired due to injury. Ron and Sylvia became Christians

Pinkus' the agents told us that a plot on Caton Road had come back onto the market which could be bought either in one or two lots, so we went to see Ron. At that time Ron was off work, ill. We asked Ron what had happened with the sale of Courtaulds on Caton Rd. Ron explained that China Clay had employed a new treasurer and this man had said to Hodgsons, 'You had half a million marked for Caton Road for nine months and nothing has happened. Now we need the money for something else.' Ron said, 'China Clay pulled the carpet from under us!' Ron advised us; 'Don't buy only one lot. Buy both lots along with the sludge pit because you'll need that for a parking area.' We returned to Pinkus' and proposed to buy the lot, plus the sludge pit for which we paid £298,000, which was £6000 less than Hodgsons had agreed to pay for it. Under Ron's directions, Hodgsons had fully mapped the area with the heights of every tree and areas of ground and the water-drainage pit. Plus, he had taken on David Sudell, a young man who had worked for our company. David was about to get married to Mary and move to Lancaster. David, along with Ron's son-in-law had already worked on the Caton Road buildings, cleaning gutters and other general maintenance. Rightly or wrongly, Ron gave us all the maps, because Hodgsons no longer needed them.

The first thing I did was to visit the manager at Courtaulds to ask him what he required of us. He replied, 'Just common courtesy.' Our business relationship worked out so well that he kindly permitted us to use his premises to access our depot because for six weeks there was no road in from the A6. The only argy-bargy I had with this manager was when I impatiently began to fill in the sludge pit before it had officially been transferred to us. They used the sludge pit to store water drawn from the River Lune in their processing. The water had to stand in the pit to allow the sand to settle on the bottom.

When Peter and I showed our wives Marian and Anne, the main building, 75,000 square feet of emptiness, they asked, 'What on earth will you put in here?' We said, 'We will find something.' To us men, an empty building of this size was impressive.

Communication and Relationship

We had to carve out a new road onto the main A6. My good friend Malcolm Hartley, a civil engineer with Lancashire County Council, drew up the plans for the access road. The firm of R.E. Leech (Ronny – the boss) were concreting the new entrance and complaining about the restrictions Malcolm was putting on them. The men moaned that they could have completed the work in only two days, but it had taken almost a week. Afterwards, Malcolm said, 'It has been done to motorway standards, David. You won't have any trouble with it in your lifetime.' He was right.

Peter and I had never done general warehousing so we brought Ron in to work for us. Now that he'd become a Christian he quickly tired of some of the methods of his CEO, and of drinking with him. He wanted a new approach to life and work.

Our idea was to put a small cabin at the entrance, to employ a girl for the office, and a fork-lift driver for the warehouse, but the whole project took off so successfully that that 'small' idea never came to fruition. We had to build bigger. There was a mezzanine floor and several offices beneath. We transformed the mezzanine floor into offices and created an office for Ron, Peter and the girls who worked for us, and of course, the canteen. Peter loves coffee! He'd always said we would have a coffee machine and coffee at hand all day. I imagined he'd buy one of these Italian bishk-booshisobish-boo thingies, but Peter lashed out £40 for a tiddly unimpressive item.

Ron got busy. He phoned Captain Pepper at Heysham Transport and asked if we could work for him. Captain Pepper needed storage for 600 tons of new potatoes from Egypt and Cyprus that January. The potatoes had to be stored under black plastic to stop light getting at them which would cause them to sprout. This was our first contract at Caton Road. In order for the bank to lend us money we had to provide projected figures for utilisation of the buildings. Ron and Peter, with me looking over their shoulders, thought that the first year we would be 50 - 75% capacity and by year two we'd be 100% full. When we checked the figures, Ron thought that it didn't look quite enough to satisfy the bank, so he added another halfpenny per square foot on, just to show what a farce the whole process was. We couldn't guarantee anything! Then it happened.

Ron contacted Bowater Scotts, who we had stored for at R.O. Hodgsons, and Scott's knew Ron's capabilities. The bosses came to inspect our premises on the Tuesday and told us, 'We do want to use you and will start next Monday.' Two days later, they asked if they could start earlier, on the Saturday. Of course we agreed.

Inside the buildings, there had been some machinery and air-ducting left which needed removing. Our drivers from Greens Farm agreed to come down on Saturday mornings to help us clean up. We would go and get fish and chips for dinner. I can still visualise them on a sunny Saturday morning, twelve men all sat against the wall eating their fish and chips the good old way, out of newspaper.

One of the buildings (approximately 10,000 sq ft) had a lot of low girder work in the roof which made it impossible for forklifts to stack anything high. An engineer from Leeches told us what steel we could take out, and which girders were essential to leave in. Now we could stack up to the roof between the girders.

Elephant Toilet Rolls and Fire

Eventually, we got the 75,000 sq ft building lifted another ten feet, so we could stack higher. In one of our buildings we stored medical paper from Cooks at Beetham. In the smaller one, we stocked giant rolls of paper, that we nicknamed, 'Elephant Toilet Rolls.' Those smallish buildings were very high. Running alongside these buildings, was a low lean-to building full of roof pipes. We turned this into a repackaging shed. When we cut the pipes off with a welding torch, unfortunately the pipes contained acetate residue from Courtauld's processing of nylon which caught fire. The fire travelled through the pipes in the wall and set some of the gigantic toilet rolls alight.

We got most of Cook's medical paper out before the firemen did the damage with their water. I know it is necessary, but the firemen often do more damage with the water than the fire does. I was walking across the yard as the fire was happening and I felt as though the Lord said, 'Hold this lightly, David.' Material things, money and business come and go. Nothing material lasts for ever. The sad result of the fire was that Cooks stopped storing with us. Thankfully Bowater Scotts were more understanding and continued to trust us.

Thieves get Flush with Toilet Rolls

Thieves struck at a Lancaster company twice within hours, cleaning it out of more than 70,000 toilet rolls. The thieves made their getaway with a trailer parked at Safegard Storage on the Lansil industrial estate, loaded with 39,000 Aldi toilet rolls. The two trailers and their stolen cargoes, which were due to be delivered to supermarkets, are valued at more than £35,000. Safegard Managing Director, Peter Gardner, said today, 'The toilet tissue will probably end up on market stalls or at car boot sales. They must have arrived with an artic and hitched up the trailers. The first was stolen between 8.30pm on Friday and I was notified just two hours before my daughter's wedding. The next was stolen between 11am on Saturday and some time on Monday morning. The toilet rolls were due to be delivered to supermarkets on Monday. We had another trailer pinched back in February when they also stole the tractor unit which ended up being abandoned in Newcastle.' Peter added, 'We even had security patrols but to no avail. I am sure this is the last time we will have a trailer stolen because we are fitting fully-automatic locking gates as soon as possible.'

The stolen trailers are described as curtain-sided, bearing the company's orange Safegard Storage logo on a red background. Anyone with information is asked to call the police on 63333.

Family

We had moved into The Hollies in Catterall, but although we lived there for eleven years, Anne, myself and the children never called it home. Whenever we talked of home, our minds took us back to Dolphinholme. We hoped one day to return there. Of course, you can't go back to the past. We must all move forward. Dolphinholme with its new buildings had changed drastically from the village we had known. The truth is that we wouldn't have wanted to be there anyway.

When we lived at the Hollies, I remember how busy Anne's life was. We often argued about time, or the lack of

Centre: My mother-in-law, Nana Phillips with Jason.
Clockwise from top left: Pip (our nephew), Jonathon,
Andrew, Timothy, Cherith, Simon, David

it, because there were so many of us under one roof, including Anne's mother and her nephew, known as Pip. Anne's brother Joe and his wife Mary had five children; Pip, Anne, Matthew, Christopher and Amanda. Joe was RAF. When he was posted to Germany, we'd let Pip live with us for two years so he could continue his schooling. In exchange they gave us a chest freezer. Cherith had to share a bedroom with her grandmother, which can't have been easy for either of them, but the rest of our children were boys! Anne's mother, Elizabeth Phillips nee Gomersall had diabetes. She eventually had to have a leg amputated. She lived with us in the Hollies for ten years. I'd carry her up and down the stairs morning and night. She used to say, "David, I envy you your strong back" Years later I ended up having two serious back operations. She died in Chorley hospital after having her second leg amputated.

From the Hollies the boys went to Bilsborough School before going to Ripley. Tim went to Castle School in Lancaster until we moved him to Ripley. All our children (and some of our grandchildren) finished up there. Andrew's wife Katharine also taught at Ripley for a few years in the 1990s.

The Hollies on Joe Lane was a lovely, big house, with a small garden in which I battled with my children. I insisted that each of them should remove ten weeds from the garden every Saturday – I could have done it quicker myself, but I never weakened. Each Monday morning Anne would sort nine piles of washing ready to go through our top-loading Hotpoint. Tuesday was ironing day.

Wednesday was baking day. We always sat down for an 11am coffee break and a 3pm coffee break – always coffee never tea. We maintained the old routine from many years ago but what happened on Thursday and Friday I haven't a clue!

One Christmas while living at the Hollies, I put my hand on the stove which left a horseshoe imprint on my hand. The smell was not of delicious turkey but nasty burnt flesh! One of our books was 'Mr Humphrey's Book of Honey' which recommended lathering honey on the wound. This we did and in about ten days it had healed. We used a hot honey poultice on Andrew to sooth a boil on the back of his neck – to this day, he has a scar from this boil.

Cornwall and Scotland
Feeding the 5000 – or was it 7?

When we lived at the shop we'd bought a new Wolsey car, but after joining the haulage world, Peter ran our finances. He told me we couldn't afford to run the Wolsey as we were still paying it off. So we traded the Wolsey for an MG 1300cc. This little car was obviously too small to take a growing family on holiday with our financial restrictions. So for one holiday, we hired a VW campervan and borrowed a bell-tent with a floor incorporated, from Pearcy's farmers. The year? I've no idea. Anne was expecting a baby, but that doesn't tell me anything about what year it was! We drove the VW to Scotland on the A74. Overnight, we parked on a wide verge on a railway bridge, so when the trains ran beneath us they woke us all up! We drove north to Gairloch. It was extremely cold. We'd planned for Anne and I to sleep in the tent with the children in the campervan, however, it was much warmer in the tent so we put the children in it while we slept in the van. At 4am we brewed tea to keep ourselves warm!

Another holiday: We stayed in Rumbling Bridge, Dollar in Scotland

At Gairloch we parked up on the shore where we saw a man and his son trying to launch a dinghy. I lent him a hand with it as it was so heavy. The man then offered me a sail in the boat. His son was not happy about this, but all the same, I accepted. We set off and the son tacked, but in anger he did it quickly and furiously, without explaining to me that he was tacking to move to the other side of the boat. The boat overturned and I swam back to the shore. I'm positive the son did it deliberately.

We exchanged our MG car for a Commer Caravette which had a Jensen body. Jensen made beautiful cattle trucks and the Caravette was superbly finished in wood. It was a bulky affair, ideal for family holidays.

Again in Scotland, we holidayed in Edinburgh. We went to Arthur's Seat, a well-known hill just beyond Holyrood. We climbed the hill. The boys all wearing fustian (thick fluffy brand new corduroys) slid down the hill on their backsides, and by the time they'd reached the foot of the hill, their trousers were smooth and shiny.

Our family usually went to Cornwall for holidays. Only once was the weather so atrocious that we returned to Lancashire after only four days. The first time we went down in the Caravette, the engine kept boiling. We took it to various garages who all suggested us different reasons for it. We had to keep the thing topped up with water. On the return journey it became impossible to continue because of over-heating. I rang Peter. We waited in Western-super-Mare in Somerset for Geoffrey and Peter to come down with the Leyland cattle truck, which was large enough to load the Caravette into. They duly arrived. Geoffrey walked straight to the Caravette, undid the cap on the radiator and removed the wax thermostat. He said, 'Now try it. The vehicle won't get warm but you will get home all right.' So he and Peter set off driving home, with our family following in the Caravette. As I told you in a previous chapter, Geoff was a fettler and a fettler mends and repairs all manner of things rather than buying new parts.

We enjoyed some breaks at Two Chimneys, Marazion. Before we departed for the holiday, Anne would spend two days cooking and preparing but then when we finally reached our destination, she'd spend two days worn out with migraine.

The annual fortnight holiday was always a priority. Our extra income was £7 cash each Saturday night plus a little family allowance on a Tuesday which paid for the break. A favourite destination was in Godrevy in Cornwall where the boys would mess about in rock pools. Because of our financial limitations we allocated £5 per day for entertainment for all of us. One summer we saw a dinghy with oars to buy for £8. We all agreed to spend an extra half day's allowance on that. We were in Mousehole and were excited as we rowed across to the 'little island', not St Michael's Mount but a pile of rocks just outside the harbour. We stayed there soon after the locals had lost the Penhale lifeboat, so there was an atmosphere of sadness.

In other years, as money became easier, we took Jonny and Jason to Trelawne Manor near Looe. The rest of the children never let us forget the fact that the youngest two had stayed in a proper hotel! For our final holiday as a family, apart from Timothy, we hired a caravan and towed it down the Lizard Peninsula. This was Andrew's last holiday with us. The children were growing up fast. All Anne and I did was open tins and feed the family. They just ate and ate. Still we enjoyed it.

The Methodist Days 1937-42 or thereabouts

Old Ma Kelly Belly was a teacher at Dolphinholme School. Her real name was Mrs Kelsall and she did not like Methodists. Not one bit. The only Methodist families in the village were the Parkinsons and us so there were very few Methodist children in the school at that time. Old Ma Kelly Belly would get easily annoyed with me and clip the back of my head. She had a ring on her finger and I could really feel it.

The Hodgsons

Dolphinholme Chapel was a new build in 1936, replacing the old congregational chapel that had been in the garden at the shop. It was like an island - people sailed to it from farmsteads and homes from miles around. One of these was a godly man called Willie Hodgson who farmed at Starbank. When, aged 17, I eventually became a Christian Willie said in his broad Lancashire accent, 'We meant to have thee converted three years ago.' And they had! Three years earlier Willie and John Townley Senior had taken me to hear an evangelist, Tom Butler from Cliff College, speaking at Caton Methodist Church. The sad thing was that even after a large group of us young people became Christians, we were so ignorant and naïve that we ignored Mr Hodgson, dismissing him as old-fashioned because he had bored us to death in Sunday school. The floor of the Sunday school was covered with rush matting so, to keep his trousers clean when he prayed, Willie would spread out his white handkerchief and kneel on it. He'd then pray for what seemed like hours! He didn't relate to us youth. I know we hurt him emotionally because we wanted a youth fellowship and we certainly didn't want him to bore us with his praying so we didn't invite him to come along. We were impetuous and foolish to shun this man of prayer from our lives. Hindsight is a wonderful thing. Charles Price, once a principle of Capernwray Hall, said, 'When I was first a Christian it felt like trying to grab a bar of soap in the bath. I couldn't quite get a hold of it properly.' I'm aware that my initial reason to become a Christian was because of fear, but later I became positive that Christianity was real and the right way to go.

Before my conversion, while at Sunday school I fought with a boy called David Close, who had begun to steal my thunder. His family had recently moved into Dolphinholme from Inglewhite, because his dad had just been killed in a tractor accident. Our Sunday school teacher was Willie Hodgson's son, Harry. Harry said he was going to 'get me' because I'd threatened David Close. So I ran home. Harry chased me, drew level with me to show that he could beat me, and then did nothing.

After I joined the army, whenever I was on leave I went to visit Mr Willie Hodgson in his home. He lived at Chapel House on the corner of Dolphinholme. After all the years I finally valued him as a man and as a spiritual mentor. One visit I found him lying in bed seriously ill. Willie looked at me with a beaming face and suddenly said, 'David, I am ready for Him to take me any time He wants.'

I was a Shocker!

Every year the Cliff Trekkers called at Dolphinholme Methodist Chapel on their way to Morecambe beach. During their mission of July 1949 Anne began to consider whether to give her life to Christ. I worried, thinking, 'What if Anne becomes a Christian and I don't?' As a teenager, I was in no way a Christian. I'd describe myself as a 'shocker!' At the end of one of the meetings Anne did go forwards to be prayed for. The very next night I also went out, but it was more out of fear of going to Hell. It was many years before I fully understood the love of God and that Christianity was not about fear. Anne, on the other hand had always loved God. Even as a child in the Roman Catholic Church she'd loved God. At this time, I was thrilled to be convinced of the truth of Christianity, even if it was through fear. I danced all the way home from church, burden gone. The following morning when I told my mother, she said, 'I can see by your face that things have changed.'

Soon after my conversion, when I was 17, I announced to Anne that I'd had a 'big flash' to become a missionary. Anne didn't worry about that at all. She just said, 'Well going on the mission field will fit in fine with me being a fever nurse.' She would never argue about things like that, probably because she was somewhat insecure. She was therefore generally content to go along with any of our shared positive ideas.

Back row, centre: Anne

When the Trekkers came in July 1968 we had such good meetings that we decided to have another evangelistic campaign the following year, from 25th January to 3rd February. Alec Passmore and Jimmy Owen, Cliff

College evangelists, came for a ten-day mission. We were praying for the success of the mission in our usual way – planning something then asking God to bless it (!) That Friday evening, two usually private men, Alec Sayer Senior and Robert Carter Senior, both prayed for the salvation of their children. It was amazing to me because these men never spoke out loud in meetings for any reason.

One of my lifelong friends is David Ollerton. He was always a bit of a character. He was 'gifted' in starting arguments on the school bus and then quietly getting off, leaving chaos to play out. He used to come into our shop and tell Mary France who worked with us, 'I can't believe in God like you people do.' David's family were C of E, so it was a surprise to everyone when David Ollerton and his mum appeared at what we called the 'Sunshine Corner' children's meeting. The children would sing the following ditty: *Sunshine Corner, oh it's jolly fine! It's for children under ninety-nine. All are welcome, seats are given free. Dolphinholme Sunshine Corner is the place for me!*

After the first night, the Ollertons turned up every night of the campaign and on the Sunday, to our amazement, David became a Christian. As we were walking home from the meeting, we stopped at the old post-office, David to go down to Common Bank Farm and me to the shop. David turned to me and said, 'You Methodists say you haven't to drink, and you haven't to smoke. I don't do it a lot. Only socially. The occasional drink and two or three cigarettes.' I had a word of wisdom from God and told him, 'We don't say we *can't* drink or smoke, we just don't want to because of the harm it does, but don't you worry about it, just leave it to the Holy Spirit.' A fortnight later, David and I went to hear the preacher Herbert Silverwood at Caldervale. Afterwards we drove back over the Wyre Bridge at Street when David said, 'Smoking and drinking - gone!'

A year after these 'missions' only a third of those new 'converts' to Christianity would continue in the faith. People often make a 'head-decision' to believe in the truth of the Bible but, as in the parable of the sower, a percentage of these will choose not to follow this up with their daily lives. *But in 1969 something different happened.* About fifteen or sixteen people were converted, including Mervyn and Mary France, John and Christine Parker, Robert and Raymond Ayrton, John Carter, Alec Sayer to name a few – and all the others I could name have continued to this day in 2016 to follow Christ consistently.

Previous to these conversions, Anne and I decided to start a youth meeting on a Saturday night but it hadn't taken off. After these events a meeting automatically began on Sunday evening in our home. Preachers came to share and not to preach. This meeting quickly grew in number. People such as Tom Parker brought along their children. This event was the beginning of what became known as the 'Upper Room Fellowship.' George Carter suggested this name as we met above the shop in our large lounge. Access was via some steps that ran up the outside of the house. Before this, the lounge had been used as a provender room, a store room for flour and other produce but it was a waste of a good space and we were able to store it elsewhere.

During the summer of 1969, I invited Mr and Mr Packham to come and share with us. They were 'way-out' Pentecostals and they started talking about the Holy Spirit. Relatively recently in 2014 I was reflecting on this with David Ollerton and Alec Sayer who told me that that night many young people began to search for the person of the Holy Spirit to empower their lives. A few weeks after the Packhams had visited, a group of young folk went to Hollybush Farm, Northallerton. Mary France had heard that God was moving in mighty ways at Hollybush so she'd gone to spend a week there. Her brother Mervyn was going to pick her up and a group of the lads said, 'We'll all come with you.' They arrived late for the final meeting and therefore had to sit on the front row. The meeting was closing and the benediction given and all this group were suddenly filled with the Holy Spirit and fell onto the floor.

Anne and I only heard about this at the following Sunday night Upper Room fellowship. Within a few minutes of us opening the meeting, all the young people were lying on the floor praising God and speaking in tongues. Anne and I sat on the sofa, baffled because we'd never seen anything like this before. I rang around the churches to try to locate our minister, Barrie Walton, who I knew had been filled with the Spirit. After ninety minutes or so, Barrie arrived. The young people were still worshipping. Barrie brought them to order and taught them that they were always in charge. He said, 'The Spirit will move you and you can know when to stop.' Barrie and Eva had already both been filled with the Holy Spirit through the ministry of Arthur Wallace.

Farmers Tom Parker and Bill France, whose sons John and Mervyn were in this group, rang me because they thought their lads had caught religious mania, saying 'hallelujah' and 'praise the Lord' as they were working on the farm. So I told them I'd arrange for them to meet another farmer, Jim Wilkinson from Hollybush. Jim agreed to come down and explain things. A week later, Jim met with these parents at our house, The Hollies in Catterall. All the young people attended. The meeting opened with introductions. Within a couple of minutes, after some prayer, young John Parker began to speak in tongues. Afterwards, Jim Wilkinson said to me, 'I'm glad it was one of *your* lads who set the meeting off in tongues.' In this way, all the parents fully grasped that God was moving in a new way with us.

Sometime after this David Ollerton arrived at Catterall one night. He said, 'I've just been to Catforth because I thought there was a meeting on, but I had decided that if it wasn't I was going to come back to you.' We were sitting in the lounge conversing quietly when David asked, 'Have you ever spoken in tongues?' and I said, 'No.' David said, 'Let's pray. Just relax and whatever comes out of your mouth let it come. I had a couple of words and it developed from there. It never became long and drawn out until after Anne had died and then quite a few more sentences developed as though God was providing comfort.

Three years later, many of us felt compelled to leave Methodism.

Leaving Methodism - the pain and the gain

We left Methodism in 1972. The Methodist church in Britain was heading towards Ecumenicalism and joining the World Council of Churches: they sent out liberal literature to our trainee preachers. David Ollerton wrote to the Local Preachers' Mutual Aid (LPMA) and asked them not to send the modernistic literature to our local preachers. They replied, 'We will make the decisions about what kind of literature we send to them.' The main trend in Methodism at that time was that it didn't matter what you believed as long as you had some kind of 'belief.' When I was at Cliff College there were two lads who were 'modernists,' who said it wasn't necessary to have the blood of the cross because it was too gory and God could have done it some other way. For us, we either believed the Bible or we didn't. It might sound simplistic to modern ears, but that was how we were.

Discussions began about withdrawing from Methodism. Uncle Joe Towers, *(see p19)* and I went to Lower Penwortham Methodist Church to meet with seven people from different Methodist churches to discuss joining the 'Voice of Methodism.' This movement began as a means to combat this new attitude from within Methodism itself. After some discussion we decided that 'Voice of Methodism' was not the right way for us. Two of our leading families, the Carters and the Townleys along with others, all agreed they would say 'No' to Methodism moving into Ecumenicalism when the time came, not realising that although many were in agreement at

Dolphinholme the numbers would be combined as only ONE vote at Synod. If our representative went to Synod and changed his mind on the very day of voting, regardless of the majority, then he could have voted for it and that would have been that. So the debate to leave Methodism continued, along with other people from churches outside the Garstang circuit. During this period, Anne and I moved to Catterall to run the cattle haulage business and there we joined Catterall Lane Methodist Chapel. This move connected me with the Garstang group who were considering leaving Methodism.

During one of the discussions at Dolphinholme Chapel, without first putting my mind in gear, (which frequently happens,) I blurted, 'We don't want people dressing up in frocks leading our worship!' Tom Hodge sent Brian Stevenson into the vestry to fetch the picture of John Wesley that showed him preaching in a gown, so I crawled under the seat – but not for long . . .

In Garstang Chapel the full circuit met to discuss this withdrawal from Methodism. The debate grew very heated. Some men who were Methodist to the core wanted to stay in Methodism. One of these, a valued local preacher, stood at the front and said, 'Let us fight from within against ecumenicalism and modernism. Let them know we are furious!' He offered this amusing illustration: *Up at Oakenclough Mill, one of the men's wives was having an affair whilst he was on nightshift. His workmates knew about it and one night they persuaded the man, on his break, to go home and check on his wife. When the man returned they asked, 'What happened?' He said, 'You were* right. *He was there in bed with her.'* The workmates asked him, *'So what did you say?'* He replied, *'I slammed t' door so they knew I was furious.'*

I now joined with the Garstang group. We met at our home, the Hollies: Geoff Chapman, Alan Ramm, Keith Whittaker, Charles Brayfield and me. In our area, we were the main leaders of the movement to leave Methodism. We had to decide whether we wanted to be connexional or independent. The vote went with connexional, meaning that we would join another denomination. Ministers who came out with us were Frank Ockenden, who was the superintendent of our circuit, with Barrie Walton as his assistant who was our area minister, also, Frank Mitchell from Morecambe, and Ron Taylor from Winstanley who had already left Methodism to be independent. (Ron Taylor already had contacts with the Free Methodists. He introduced us to Victor Trinder from Northern Ireland, who was connected with Free Methodism, an American denomination rooted in Wesleyan teachings.)

Barrie, Ron, and Frank had looked into Free Methodism and we all accepted it after Barrie became our pastor. My own dad also became a Free Methodist - one result of this was that he chose to stop smoking. Another older person, Mrs Fenton, our organist, who ran a shop opposite the high school at Bowgrave, stopped selling cigarettes. At one of the services in Cabus Village Hall, my parents asked Pastor Barrie to baptise them. They were in their seventies. Barrie got a bowl of water from the kitchen and baptised them in the hut. This was our church building - a wooden hut with a rotted hole in the floor at one end!

This was another sign of God working by His Holy Spirit because previously we had known nothing of adult baptism.

We were eventually sworn in to Free Methodism, in Dolphinholme Village Hall. Back then we did accept the rule of no drinking and no smoking. We might have been naïve but we accepted this easily as it was already part of the Methodist way of thinking. However, I used to say, 'It's illogical! You can beat your wife and kick the cat, as long as you don't smoke or drink.'

Dolphinholme Methodists came to join us in Garstang, along with the Catterall group and others from Bilsborough. There was an air of expectancy. We prayed to God, asking what we should do next.

Whilst we were still in Methodism a group of us used to hold an open-air service on a Sunday evening, situated where the mini roundabout is opposite what is presently Sainbury's in Garstang. It was by the bridge as you come into Garstang from the south. After the meeting we'd go into the Methodist Chapel for a brew, to chat with inquirers. But after we left Methodism, Garstang Chapel people stopped us using their premises so we transported people in cars to Crown Lane. A group of our young people such as the Frances and the Ayrtons were filled with the Spirit and got into a holy huddle speaking in tongues and praising God. One lad became scared and climbed out of the toilet window. I had to advise them to be controlled, to be orderly as the Bible teaches. I remember Mary France saying to me, 'Hallelujah anyway,' and I said, 'Mary, it is not hallelujah anyway.' By that I meant that we needed to be in order.

"Let all things be done decently and in order."
1 Corinthians 14 v 40

After we left Methodism, Mervyn France and the Ayrton family decided to emulate Hollybush so they transformed a granary at Kays Farm, Over Wyresdale, into a building for worship. This became known as the 'Kays Farm Fellowship'. People arrived from near and far to attend the Monday night meeting. Initially, the people there tried to remain within Methodism but when they learnt that their new freedom in worship was not welcomed by the denomination, sadly they were forced to break away.

We Free Methodists began to look for places to worship. As forementioned, the Garstang community met in the wooden hut in Cabus. The Porter family, farmers at Great Eccleston, gave us a piece of land just off Hall Lane on which the Great Eccleston church was constructed, one of the first Free Methodist buildings in the north west.

We at Garstang were looking for a place or some land. We checked out a house on Lancaster Road with a large room upstairs that could hold about forty people. Our new superintendent Victor Trinder advised against it, much to my chagrin. I was desperate to get going. But Victor was wise. The piece of land that we ended up buying was God-given. The council had had an eye on this plot on Windsor Road, Garstang for two or three different developments so we thought we stood no chance to get it.

However, we were able to buy it and God blessed us as people became Christians and others joined us because they enjoyed the freedom in worship. One of the most notable things was the presence of God and love in the place. I believe God blessed us at this time, because for the first time in our lives we were constantly asking God, 'Where to and what to next?'

After we'd got established on Windsor Road, a small group of Christians who had also attended the Methodist Church but had been part of the breakaway, worshiped with us there. Mr and Mrs Woods were in this group. When Mrs Woods in particular prayed, she took you straight into God's presence. Mr Woods was a retired dentist and one of the leaders of the breakaway movement. When we were deciding whether we could afford to employ Barrie Walton as our pastor, we were discussing this and Mr Woods gave us all a piece of paper and an envelope and said, 'Write down privately what you can afford to give each week.' He opened each envelope on the top of the piano, counted the contents and the total came to £32!' This meant we could employ a pastor. (Our drivers were on £14.50 per week).

Before our services, Mrs Fenton would play the organ and we'd sing for twenty minutes before the preacher stood in the pulpit. But Mr and Mrs Woods and a group of like-minded people were not so keen on this. They called that time, 'Mrs Fenton's half hour,' with reference to a BBC programme that was called *somebody or other's* half hour of music. We were moving in the things of the Spirit like never before, becoming more like the Pentecostal movement. Our pastor, Barrie, in respect for these lovely people, put the brakes on a bit but later he commented, 'We grieved the Spirit. I will never, ever put the brakes on again.' Garstang Church has not yet returned to that place of freedom that we experienced but historically, these things do rise and fall, and there will be times of reviving. The church at Garstang grew and within a few years we had to extend the building to accommodate the increase in attendance.

For the sake of history – some extra information

Back in 2011 - 12 the Rev Dr Derek Tidball wrote a paper on the Origin of the Free Methodist Church. He wrote to me about this. Excerpts from our correspondence follows:

7th December 2011 From myself to Derek

Gillows Green, Clifton Hill, Forton, Preston PR3 0AQ

Dear Derek,

Son number 5, Jon, is doing a course at Nazarene, Manchester and brought home Wesley and Methodist Studies Vol. 3 for me, so I could read your article on secession from Methodism to Free Methodism. Whilst our move to Free Methodism was ministerially led, many of us were already on the move. Barrie [Walton] and Frank [Mitchell] both had congregations to go to. Ron [Taylor] was already established at Winstanley.

I'm not writing this from any personal pride but knowing God was doing a new thing with a section of His people. I was at Dolphinholme when it first started, at a local preacher's meeting. A year before this, we had sent a letter to the head office telling them not to send any more 'modernistic and liberal theological books' to our local preachers in training. Head office replied, 'We will be the ones to decide what literature to send out.' We were very uncomfortable with this. The older folk at Dolphinholme Methodist Church said, 'When the time comes we will each vote 'no' to this, but they did not realise their combined vote only amounted to the single vote of our delegate to the conference.

Our family moved to Catterall for business reasons, but this meant moving to Catterall Methodist Church. Church leaders in Garstang and Catterall met to discuss what to do after we left Methodism; to go independent or to join a connexion. Out of the 5 of us, 2 voted for independence and 3 for connexion. I was later to be glad of this decision.

118

Then some of met in our home to discuss whether we could afford to ask Barrie to be our pastor. One of the elders, Mr Woods, suggested we all wrote down a figure of money that we could afford to give weekly. The total came to £32, so we knew we could afford to pay Barrie properly. (At that time our drivers were on £15 per week). We asked Barrie, who agreed, but surprised us by saying he was also going to pastor Great Eccleston and Woodplumpton in Catforth, so we formed a central committee which ran for the next 8 years.

Now to the important theme of "God doing a new thing." By now Dolphinholme and a couple of other churches had joined us. We met in an old wooden hut, Cabus Village Hall. We learned about tithing, full-immersion baptism and moving in the Holy Spirit, both the fruit and the gifts. It was a wonderful time. Most of us were saying, "Lord, where do we go from here?" Great Eccleston Church was built first, then a farmhouse at Crown Lane was adapted for church worship, then Garstang was built, and then Fulwood on the sight of the old Silver Hill Farm. We became separate congregations or churches.

Derek, I hope I have not bored you. They were wonderful times. I am sounding the old man that I am! There was so much that God did in our midst, I wish I could really write . . .
Yours in the name of Christ Jesus
David Gardner

22nd January 2012 From Derek by email

Dear David
Thank you for your email. I'm probably going to write a wider piece on the challenge to evangelicalism in several denominations in the late 60s reviewing what happened to the Methodists and the Baptists at the time. It is good to have contact with your family. Yesterday, Dianne and I began the day praying in a small group with Cherith. On Thursday I was with Rachel all day at the EA [Evangelical Alliance] and I suspect I might see Jason at LICC [London Institute of Contemporary Christianity] tomorrow. What a wonderful influence your family exercise for Christ. Blessings and best wishes
Derek

A letter from Derek Tidball, Glen Parva, Leicester [undated]

Dear David

How good it was to hear from you. It was kind of you to write and I am very grateful for the information you included. You make a very valid point about the lay involvement in the origins of Free Methodists. I will make some slight revisions in my article, due to be published again in a book of essays on evangelicalism sometime next year by Oxford University Press.

I wish you were able to write things up. I would encourage you not to destroy any papers you have as they will be useful at some stage. If you are unable to write the story, maybe record some of it on a cassette or disk?

I'm not sure if I will ever be able to do it, but I would love to write about it more fully at some stage as I do think FM is a very significant part of our evangelical history. I keep hoping I might clear other tasks to devote some time to it.

I was recently in West Cornwall and wherever I went I picked up that while others struggle, your churches down there are doing well. Given the hand you had in their founding you'll be encouraged that God is still blessing the work.

It's good to see several of your children from time to time, and of course, to be in the same church as Cherith. I waved at her across the church just yesterday but sadly didn't get a chance to speak. I always ask after you.

Thank you for your encouragement. May God provide you with joy, health and strength in these days.

Blessings in Christ
Derek

Spanish Days

We had closed the Burscough Depot. Jimmy Miller who had taken over from Andrew running Burscough had come back to work at Greens Farm. The office was somewhat crowded. I was taking Tramadol all day just to keep me going. One Friday morning Peter came in and said, 'I think you should retire.' He had obviously talked this over with my son David, aged 29 who was working for us. I wasn't well, so even though I felt awful I was also greatly relieved. I went home to Rivendell and said to Anne, 'They've sacked me!' Ending work was a real shock but we knew it was for the best.

I went to see Chris Faux, an orthopaedic surgeon at Preston. Chris and his wife Patty had become friends of ours, because, whilst we were at the Hollies, Anne had worked two days a week, cleaning for Patty who was a radiologist at Blackpool. One evening they came to Rivendell for a meal. The next day Patty commented to Chris on how lovely it had been to go home from a social event and not to have to hang their clothes in the window to remove the smell of tobacco and wine! This couple were good friends of ours, such that when Jonny had an ear operation in Blackpool, Patty rang Anne every hour throughout the five-hour procedure, to reassure her that everything was going well. Sadly, we lost touch with Chris and Patty.

During my first back operation, Chris removed a slipped disc and this was reasonably successful. Chris advised me to get a fortnight in the sun so Anne and I went to a place in Mijas, Spain that had been bought by two brain surgeons from New York. The garden had not yet been fully developed but there was a swimming pool. There was a short, sharp hill up to the car park to get to the house. It didn't do my back much good walking up and down this hill.

One Sunday morning I went to phone my brother Peter in England to say we'd arrived in Mijas safely. He said, 'You'll be having your own little service this morning,' but I told him I'd just walked past an English-speaking church and decided to try it. We went there at 11am and there we met Theo and Charlotte who became our close friends. They were widowers who had married each other, and have since been married for over 30 years.

When we were in our holiday cottage, we put our coats in the cloakroom cupboard. The door jammed. It was

totally stuck. I rang the agent and said, 'Help. What do I do if it rains?' He said, 'You go out and dance in it like everyone else.' Theo and Charlotte used to do their washing at 4am because the water in the area would run out later in the day.

A beautiful Spanish evening

Peter suggested that while we were out there we could look for a place to buy as a holiday cottage. We explored a marina near

Puerto Banus where the Arabs parked their boats and found what we thought was a suitable place, but when Peter and Marian flew out to look at it they learnt that there were plans to develop the area opposite it, so instead they bought an apartment at Calahonda. The following August, Anne, myself and Jason went out to furnish this new apartment. The agent, David, who'd sold us the property accompanied us to buy furniture. A lad with only one eye showed us round. He was an ex light-weight boxer from Wales. Then a girl muscled in to try to show us round. I was attempting to get the best price I could, when I realised these agents were getting a 10% cut of whatever we spent. We continued without their 'help' to choose our own bedlinen.

It was costly for our adult children to fly out with their families – even the 2-year-olds had to be paid for. We hadn't thought it out sufficiently. All the same, many friends and family went and enjoyed lovely holidays there. Once, Anne flew out with four of her friends. When I retired, Peter gave me Calahonda as part of my retirement fund. We eventually sold the place for £54,000. We had been cheated out of £10,000 by the Calahonda directors. We had to pay tax on the difference between the £24,000 they had put on the books with the purchase of Calahonda, where in actual fact we'd paid £34,000. The agent who sold it for us explained that Calahonda directors had often been dishonest with the figures, knowing that because (obviously) everything was in Spanish, we couldn't understand the documents properly. After Calahonda sold, we began to look for a place in France.

We'd known Ernie Kidd, of Kidd's haulage, all our lives. He and his wife Edwina had an apartment in St Pedro, Spain. We visited them and found St Pedro to be like the Wild West in the USA. The seafront was rough and horrible. The esplanade stretched for over a mile towards the sea, passing through a dreary, dusty, scruffy area. St Pedro had received some renovation funding from Europe - they'd used the money to build the esplanade using beautiful tiles, right through this barren place. Crazy! They'd also built a motorway which included a toll that the locals were unable to use. The Kidds also owned a 40-footer yacht that Edwina didn't much care for, because as she said, 'We are always scrubbing decks.'

Rivendell 1987

Jason named our new home 'Rivendell' because he, along with some of my other sons, were keen Tolkien addicts. It all began when we heard about the sale of Homestead, a piece of land on which stood a small wooden house with an asbestos tiled roof and asbestos lined walls for waterproofing. This was situated just above Street. (Street is a Roman name; in fact, there is a Roman bridge as part of a wall that remains on the river bank just below where the road bridge is now. A family called the Cooksons used to live there, and, as children, my lads used to go up snigging, lifting stones and catching small eels, in the brook with the Cooksons' grandchildren. Doreen Cookson used to fry them and they'd be still wriggling in the pan while she was cooking them.

Anne had become interested in moving house. She blamed her unrest on my complaining about the noise of the trains at Haverhill. True, I had kept mentioning the trains as they passed, but it really did not bother me at all. I love trains, to the point that I've had three large-sized train sets in all, in their own rooms. My last one was eight-foot square: I built it in the garage at Gillows Green which is now our living room.

Anyway, Anne and I went up to look at the land and liked it, but discovered that Sadie Wilson nee Yates, who had been my sister Betty's great friend all her life, had already sold the plot at auction and we were too late. The plot had been purchased by a builder called Dewhurst from Longridge with his girlfriend's money paying the deposit. For some reason we said to Sadie, 'If for any reason it falls through, we'd be interested.' There was absolutely no reason for it to fall through. One week later, we heard from Sadie that although Dewhurst had paid the deposit he'd dropped out of the deal and we were welcome to buy Homestead for the last bid of £25,000.

My brother Peter looking at it, said, 'Whatever you do, you should get the piece of land with the brook in it, down to Street.' I asked Sadie about this and she said, 'Yes, you can have that bit of land for about £2000.' I asked the Yates to include two or three yards of their field so we could fence the land off and put a path around it. We also added two bridges over the brook so it became a nice circular walk. Homestead became ours.

Before building commenced, Anne and I would go up and have a look at what we'd bought. Strangely, each time we opened the car door at Haverhill, our dog and our Siamese cat Simba would jump in, go up with us to the Homestead, get out and walk around the land, and then the cat and dog would get back in the car to go back to Haverhill. We sold Haverhill and the buyers wanted to move in straightaway, so we purchased an old mobile home for £800 which we put on the Homestead site, and connected it to the water system. It had a bathroom and seven radiators which ran from a little coal fire. After the plumber had repaired seven leaks it all worked perfectly. The electrician hooked us up to the electricity. We put a small towing caravan at the end for Jonny and Jason to live in. (We hadn't yet managed to get these two married off yet!) Jason was still at school and ended up studying for his GCSEs from the caravan!

We put pallets around the caravans so we could walk on them in wet weather. We placed straw bales all around to stop the wind blowing underneath and to protect the washing machine that we'd sited outside. Previously, most Sundays, our married children would gather for tea around our table, but now Anne and I hoped that we'd get invited out to *their* homes. However, the lure of the caravan was too much and for our first Sunday there were nine extras sitting around on the floor, for tea. We enjoyed it. It was great.

*

I rang the fire brigade and asked them if they'd be interested in burning down Homestead as a training experience one way or the other, but got the curt reply, 'No, we put out fires. We don't light them.' We removed the asbestos off the outside of the house but forgot about the roof tiles being made of the asbestos. This became interesting when we set fire to the place. As they burnt they popped as loudly as fireworks. Nearly all the family had gathered to watch the burning of Homestead. It burnt rapidly. I was in one particular room and David was in another setting fire to it, and I heard David shouting, 'Dad, get out quick. Get out!' The furniture had gone up in a flash! Andrew who was videoing the whole thing said, 'From start to finish, the whole thing burnt to the ground in 20 minutes.' All that remained was the two brick built

After the fire: Anne – imagining Rivendell

chimney stacks. I was frightened at one stage, because the flames were so large they'd consumed some branches of an oak tree across the road.

We asked Roy Whiteside to build for us. One night there was a fierce wind. It blew a section of the new build down. The roof trusses hadn't been properly inserted because they'd been styled by the architect Graham Anthony in a different way than usual. He'd done special trusses in the corners to carry the weight, but because Roy Whiteside was at odds with the architect over an unrelated matter, he hadn't communicated with him concerning the structure of the house. With reference to this, a structural engineer (who later came swimming at our new pool), after I'd asked him if the cracks appearing upstairs were normal drying out or something different, questioned me, 'Where are your roof trusses?' The rafters were in but no trusses. The following Saturday, Roy Whiteside and the joiner, Derek Green, met with the engineer to discuss the matter and I asked Roy and Derek when they'd be coming to sort it out. They said, 'Monday morning.' So it was done.

Outside Rivendell in the Daimler Double Six

Inside a year, Rivendell was complete, swimming pool and all. We sold the mobile caravan to the aforesaid engineer who was doing a barn conversion at Street Farm.

We were always glad that Rivendell was well used by family, friends and church groups. Many people turned up to swim or to have church or family picnics. Pastors fraternal meetings were held each month. Various US Free Methodist bishops stayed with us. Alpha groups used us for their away days. Anne and I used to buzz off for the day and leave them to it.

When we were building, Eva Walton said, 'You'll have to build a prophet's room, David,' with reference to Elisha (2 Kings 4 v 10). A fortnight after we'd moved in, Jim Wilkinson of Hollybush fame knocked on the door at about 5pm and said, 'I believe you have a prophet's room. Can I make use of it?' We said, 'Yes.' He had his evening meal and slept the night in our 'prophet's room.'

We had a great 16 years at Rivendell. I think the majority of my grandchildren learnt to swim in our pool. We especially remember Charis, aged 2, in her little black swimming costume. I christened her "Tadpole." We still smile about the day she took off of her own accord, aged 2¼, to swim a width unaided. The adults watching all held their breath because her head was under water as she did the doggy paddle. We were delighted when Charis succeeded, but shocked when she ignored our applause, turned around and swam back again.

Les Vacances and On Not Parleying Le Francais Proper Like

Anne and I towed a caravan through France searching for a suitable property to buy. We spent two or three days just outside Poitiers. A female agent drove us miles to view a potential place, but it was rubbish. We'd looked around several houses just outside Poitiers but none were satisfactory.

Finally, we went to Chalais. The agent explained there were very few places below our maximum price bracket of £50,000 but he showed us one at Saint-Laurent-Des-Combes costing a mere £19,000. The boss of the company was very surprised that we bought it because it needed a lot doing, such as re-roofing, but we liked it. The agent who sold us this house introduced us to a flyboy who could speak a bit of English. This boy did a few repairs around the place. We discovered later that we'd been very fortunate, because this agent had got the sack for running off with the deposits that other people had put down on their properties. He must have liked us!

In the front garden was a huge willow tree. We asked the boy to cut it back and he gave us a price; '100 euros!' There was that much wood in it, it took three lorry loads to dispose of. The boy said, 'Next time you want the willow tree cutting down, ask someone else.' A local builder, Robert Montabaun, who used a barn nearby, was a lovely guy. Anne's brother Joe, who used the cottage a lot, always addressed him as 'Montabaun' which annoyed Anne because it didn't seem properly respectful.

Back home in England we had to follow all the new EU rules but, to my mind, the French ignored many rules and continued doing whatever they wanted to. At Chalais market the vendors cooked meat in the street and sliced it using the same knife as the uncooked meat. They used the same spoon that served the meat, to dish gravy into bags.

The village of Saint-Laurent-des-Combes was beautiful. The surrounding district of farmland and pretty villages were amazing. Owls perched in 13th century church behind the house. Some years later, because of the travelling distance we moved to Brittany but I wish we'd never moved – we hadn't thought the matter through. We always loved the house in the south. All our families and many others enjoyed holidays there.

Within a short drive were several rivers with sandy beaches. When we visited one May we saw the sand piled up at Aubeterre ready for spreading for the summer visitors. The French know how to look after their people! I believe that one result of the French Revolution was that every village and town revolved around a healthy community life. Sadly, nowadays the locals suffer because they gave themselves *too* much, such as holidays, shorter working hours and early retirement. In these days of austerity, the government has to battle to change the laxer attitudes to work.

St Aulaye is a stunning place, as is Aubeterre. Mum and Julie particularly loved the marvellous gift shop there. And the puppet theatre in the square was popular with all our families. Anne and I were disappointed when we visited some prehistoric caverns and there was no English guide – the information was all in French. I'm thinking that in Cornwall, when tourists visit the tin mines, all the guides speak in English as well as French.

Anne and I liked to go to Cognac. As the name Cognac implies there was a huge distillery for producing Cognac. The river and the town was so beautiful. We also loved nearby Jarnac. Another time we crossed the Massif Centrale to Lyons and Chamonix where Malcolm and Kaye were staying in a ski studio which was so small that, had we stayed with them, we'd have been stepping over each other to go to the toilet in the night - so we booked into a hotel. We all went to Turin in Italy, entering by one tunnel and returning through the St Bernardo tunnel. I wish we had come over the pass, because the tunnel was terrible - filthy, dirty concrete because of all the lorries and other vehicles that ran through it.

We eventually moved from St Laurent to a village called Cargo in Brittany. We had seen an advert for this house and were sent the pictures, and because we had already seen so many French properties, we said we would have it sight unseen. As we had planned to go to France the following weekend, we asked if we could view our new property. On arrival we got the keys from our lovely neighbour. Afterwards we asked her, 'Can we use your telephone' - in Franglais because she spoke English! We phoned the owners who lived in England, confirmed we would have it and that I'd send the deposit the next day. So sealed the deal. In English pounds it cost £76,000. At that time, to buy a house in UK of the same quality with the garden, would have been £400,000. We named the new house 'Davanne' - exactly the same as our previous French house. Again, the local lakes and beaches were great, as well as some splendid towns. Our favourite place was Dinan, so every time we went to Cargo, we'd go to Dinan to sit in the square to drink coffee or share a meal.

Our family visited en masse! Jonny once took 14 friends on holiday there and the drains couldn't cope! The septic tank overflowed and Jonny had to spend several hours working with the excellent local handyman, Rogert, until things flowed again. The vendors had assured us they'd just installed a new family-sized septic tank but obviously it wasn't intended for 14 people. One day, the lady next door came to speak to me. She held up her hands and said, 'Il fait beau!' I replied, 'Oui, il fait beau.' She carried on chattering in French. I had to say, 'Excusez Madam, no comprendez Francais.' She immediately said, 'Vous comprendez Francais.' ('You *will* learn French!') I used to get in trouble in shops because I was cheeky to the assistants, telling them they should speak English. They'd retort, 'But Monsieur, you are in France now. Here we speak French.' Bon.

In the flush of funds after being bought out by TDG, we purchased a beautiful chalet on the shores of Bassenthwaite. It was nice but too dear. It cost us £70 – 80 pounds per week all year and closed 4 months of the year. Every winter, for insurance purposes, we had to pay to drain all the water out and then pay to refill it in the spring. Robbers!

The Grandchildren

At Rivendell with 12/16 of our grandchildren

Anne and I took our oldest grandchildren, Alex and Susanna, (both aged 9) to Futuroscope in Poitiers. It was a very modern cinema experience. For example, we sat in a simulator 'mine' in which a runaway ore cart raced downhill. Every so often a section of railway was missing. It was terrifying, made all the more real by the hydraulic seats. In another room everyone stood around the sides of a room and we felt as if we were aboard a sailing ship. It was so realistic, as if we were actually racing over the sea! While we stayed at the Ibis, we ate our first meal together. Susanna insisted on trying escargot with her beef-burger, but when she saw it, she quickly put it on one side of her plate. It didn't crawl there! Both the girls' burgers were pink in the middle because I didn't know *bien cuit s'il vous plait* (French for well-cooked please) so the burgers were raw. The girls loved the holiday. If our initial ideas had happened, over the years we would have happily taken eight trips abroad with all the grandchildren, in pairs. These two grand-daughters inherited the Christian faith, and decided to follow it for themselves. Alex married Phil Sayer. They have a son, Zebediah (Zeb) with a new baby due at the end of 2016. Susanna married a Yorkshireman, Mark Shotter. Their sons are Joel and Samuel.

*

Luke 'helping' me

Our grandsons, Luke and Zak, used to help me out in the garden. I realised all my grandsons cost me money as they worked. I once asked Zak and Luke to remove some rubble, to wheel it out of my garden and into Geoffrey Whittaker's field gateway, because it would help firm up the ground as it was low and wet. To get out of our drive they have to cross a cattle grid. I looked out of the window and saw Luke tipping a barrow of gravel into the cattle grid. I immediately accosted him with, 'What the heck do you think you are doing?' He replied, 'Zak shouted to me to tip it there!' It would have taken far too long for them to remove it, so the gravel is still there to this day. Having grandsons to help me garden cost me quite a bit. Those lovely lads used axes as hammers, and weighed on spades to dig things out. I had to replace two axe shafts and two spade shafts.

The Delight of Daisy and on Almost Being Arrested

Jason and Rachel invited me to Harrow, London, for Daisy's special day, the day on which she officially became a member of the Gardner family and received a certificate from a judge in the family court. The certificate reads 'This is to say on this special day, that Daisy Georgia Anne becomes an official member of the Gardner family.'

Myself, Daisy and her dad Jason

It was a great experience. The judge was not in robes, but she said, 'You will want to take photographs,' and she changed into her robes to make it look official. Also present were Rachel's parents Charles and Lynne, and Rachel's friend, Katy Hall, and Daisy's social worker. As we entered the court we were searched. All metal objects and other things were put into a tray, by a policewoman. My Swiss army knife which I had recently purchased in Scotland was removed. The police lady said, 'You will get it back afterwards, sir, but we can't allow you to go in with it.' A nosy policeman lent over and picked up the knife. He pulled open the blade which locked in position. Immediately the man told me I was in possession of a locking blade – illegal to take into any court. 'But,' I insisted, 'I only use it for gardening!' He confiscated it and said, 'Sir, you shouldn't have this on your person. You won't get it back.' He reassured me that he wouldn't arrest me for my crime.

Many years ago I did have to go to court when I was in the army. My friend, Graham, had a Norton TT bike. You had to put it in gear and run very fast to get it started. I borrowed it to go to Perth, with my good friend Reg riding pillion. Going around a bend, we leant over too far and Reg fell off, hurt his ankle and ended up in hospital. I had to report the accident. The police put me up before a highly qualified Scottish judge. I arrived with two licences, a civil license and an army license. The judge looked down his nose at me saying, 'I can't make anything of these.' He let me off. He obviously wasn't bothered.

Driving Billy Graham

At the time I had a BMW 700, a lovely car. Peter suggested I could use it for chauffeuring for the Billy Graham team at Blackpool. I chauffeured the speaker Cliff Barrows and his wife Billie to their meetings. Anne and I invited them to Rivendell for lunch, then we drove them around the Trough of Bowland, to see the beauty of Lancashire. On the last night, we were taking the team to Manchester airport to the hotel for an overnight stay. When I got to my car, Billy Graham (the evangelist) was sitting in the front passenger seat! I set off. Billy said, 'Slow down to 50 mph and see what it's like for us in America!' This I did for all of 10 seconds. We arrived well before the other three cars, one of which was being driven by John Johnson (from Garstang Free Methodist Church). When they arrived, Billy asked, 'Where've you been?' When we were booking in, Billy asked the receptionist for the largest bed they had in the hotel and I was thinking, 'Oh, these big Americans,' when Billy turned to me and said, 'I'm fed up of sleeping in bed with my feet hanging over the end.' He was about 6 foot 4 inches. We had a drink and snack together.

Sometime later, I went to Gloucester in this same car, to visit my cousin, 'Young Violet.' Her mother had also been christened Violet, so her daughter was always referred to as 'Young Violet' – and she is going strong at 94 years old to this day. She is bright as a button! (Her husband was Canon Philip Hobbs, a prison chaplain in Gloucester.) When she saw my BMW, Young Violet asked, 'Please may I sit in the seat where Billy Graham sat?'

How I Ended Up Pastoring Some Churches

1990: I retired aged 58 years. After one of my back operations, Barrie approached me to ask if I'd consider pastoring the church at St Anne's. For various reasons that I won't admit to, I didn't think I was fit to be a pastor, so I said no. Then in 1991 Ken Leech, who pastored Helston Church in Cornwall and was supported by 'Light and Life Men' in the USA, had to go to USA to raise funds, which is the reason why the Cornwall Churches go under the banner of 'Light and Life.' Ken said, 'We need someone to cover while I am away.' In his prayer time the name David Gardner came into his mind. When Barrie told me this, I couldn't ignore it, because it was the second time of being asked, plus the fact that Ken and I didn't particularly know each other, so I believed it was a 'God thing'.

Pastor John Townley and myself

1991 March, April and May: I agreed to go to Cornwall for three months. Then in the October, a church in Acton Green (London) asked the Free Methodist Church to take it over so Ken Leech and his wife, Joan, went there to work for a while. As a result, Barrie asked me if I'd go and pastor Cornwall for two years. I replied that I would go for only one year because I thought I'd cope with a honeymoon year, but I wasn't confident enough to take it on for two years. As it turned out it was right for me to only do the one year because John Townley became the Pastor at Helston and we returned to Lancashire.

To backtrack a little: In the November of 1991 Anne and I departed Rivendell for Cornwall for the second time that year. The church there had been such a blessing to us in the spring, as I had been their first lay pastor experiment! That December, knowing the church was £7,000 in debt, I knew I had to confront the people with this. I was inadvertently prompted to do this by a couple whose baby had been miraculously healed. One evening, as they were leaving the church, they put some money in the offering box. I knew the treasurer had emptied the box already. I took the box to the treasurer and tipped it out. The couple had put in 20p. This sparked an idea in me. The following Sunday I talked about our finance, beginning by considering that some pastors might avoid this subject for fear that the congregation would think it is about their wages. I wasn't being paid so this didn't concern me. I said, 'It is no good putting 50p into the box and expecting heating, lighting and a pastor to serve you the following Sunday.' I continued, 'We are £7000 in debt. We are going to borrow the money from the Free Methodist conference (interest free) and it will take us 8 or 9 years to clear this debt.'

In January, after the evening service, farmers Ken and Francis Jenkins asked if they could see me the next morning. They arrived at the manse with two cheques saying, 'We believe the Lord wants us to pay the debts and by the time you get the gift aid back, the full £7000 will be cleared.' It sealed my ministry. I had been prompted, then preached a tough subject, then this happened and I realised God was in control. I was here for a reason. Another result of this event was that we discovered that Helston had never claimed any money from Gift Aid, simply because the treasurer hadn't understood how to do it. I invited Allan Ellershaw to come to preach. His wife Sue accompanied him and spent time helping the treasurer sort out the Gift Aid situation.

My friend Alan Williamson's sister-in-law, Sheila Beardswood, was working in Thailand. She had to come home but had no money for her flight. The time came for her flight and she cried because she couldn't pay for it. She said, "The Lord told me to stop crying and start praising Him, which I did. Suddenly, someone knocked at the door. In their hand was an envelope with enough money for the flight." This is a similar story to the time when I was in Cornwall and the Jenkins came with £7000 to clear the debt on the manse. These people all walked with God.

We learnt how to gift aid. Soon we were able to put a cabin on the back of the church and hold all our meetings in St John's. This saved us the weekly £25 cost of hiring the social centre for Sunday school. We held two classes in the cabin and one in the kitchen. We used the cabin for prayer and other meetings. Now we could afford to remove the choir pews and reconstruct the front of the church to create a more open space with room for activities.

One Saturday afternoon, as we were removing the rubble from the back of church in order to erect this cabin, a man handed me a brown paper bag. I opened it and inside was a bobble hat in Cornish rugby colours. The man said, 'This is to remind you that you got us round here, digging this rock, while Cornwall are playing Durham in a rugby final.' I replied, 'Why didn't you tell me? We could have postponed it.' I kept that hat in the back window of my Merc for a few years after that and I treasured it.

Other Fond Memories of this Time

Anne and her friend, Jenny Tiddy, used to heckle during the notices. They'd correct me if I got anything wrong. They'd laugh, 'No, it's not Wednesday, it's on Tuesday!' I'd been there only a fortnight when a young man approached me to say, 'I didn't know you could laugh in church until you came.'

Anne used to sing soprano and Jenny alto and the whole church enjoyed harmonising. It was tremendous. A favourite hymn was by Wesley with music by Thomas Merritt, a miner who composed many tunes for Christmas carols. The harmonies were amazing. A year later, on my birthday, I was given a CD of some of the congregation singing it for me.

That Wooden Spoon!

January 1992: I was in church, telling a children's story from 1 Corinthians chapter 12 about our body is composed of many parts all working together. Jenny Tiddy had lent me an armful of kitchen instruments which I showed to the children asking what each item was for. I held up a wooden spoon and said, 'What is *this* for?' The children shouted, 'Stirring!' and 'Mixing!' A voice from behind the piano shouted out, 'That is not what it was used for in our house.'

We often went to the beach on a Saturday afternoon with the church folk. If I tried to tell you all our happy memories from these months, you'd never reach the end of this book! As our time in Cornwall approached its end, Mervyn France drove the work's van down to help us transport all our furniture - and Anne - back home to Lancashire. I continued working in Helston for one more month, staying with our friends Terry and Jenny Tiddy in Porthleven. Anne returned to Cornwall for our final meetings with the Helston congregation as John took over in 1994.

During our time in Cornwall, we had prayed for two men, Alan Bray and Colin Simmons, hoping they'd become Christians. Ten years later in 2002, John Townley asked me to go down to help the church folk buy a site and sort out a building. When I arrived I realised that Alan Bray was the worship leader and Colin Simmons was another leader in the church. This was very encouraging. We located a site on the Water-Ma-Trout trading estate. At that time, the Helston Church met in the local primary school which needed the church to vacate the school building for about a month, because they were removing asbestos. So although the new church premises weren't ready, we decided to use it for those three Sunday services.

In Water-Ma-Trout Anne kept saying, 'Why don't use you use the building that is there?' (And this is exactly what happened some six years later.)

Carnforth

1996: I joined the leadership team at Carnforth for 19 months. Carnforth Free Methodist Church had begun as a plant from Lancaster Free Methodist Church during my son Andrew's time as pastor. Allan Ellershaw asked if Anne and I could attend Carnforth, not as a lay-pastor, but because I was a local preacher Allan wanted me to be on their board because there was only one other established Free Methodist person on it. So we attended for 19 months and enjoyed making friends there. Some years later Margaret Valentine, who had been the secretary when I was at Carnforth, said, 'We never expected you and Anne to leave us.' I felt sorry, so I apologised.

At one of the board meetings, Graham Stanford (the man who started SportsReach and was a lecturer at Capernwray College) said, 'We need an evangelistic team this summer.' I said, 'Graham, everyone is not an evangelist but we all must be a witness.' Afterwards, the treasurer Anne Knowles wrote and thanked me for telling the truth. We are not all the same. Otherwise you are trying to do something you can't. Evangelists are natural at witnessing because they are gifted. Not everyone is the same but that is not an excuse for not being a witness. We enjoyed our time and loved the folk at Carnforth.

Great Eccleston

1999 – 2001 I was privileged to pastor Great Eccleston. The congregation seemed to be in the doldrums for reasons best left unsaid. I went to Allan Ellershaw and offered, 'If Great Eccleston are willing, then I think I can help.' It was amazing to me that these people were my peers who had left Methodism with us, yet they let me lead them as their pastor. I asked if we could run an Alpha course not as an evangelistic effort, but to bond the church people together again. I suggested we did it in the evening. About 36 people arrived. The food was good. We started at 6.45pm to allow for late-comers, so they could be on time, but they were late just the same! Alpha did bring the people together. Kathleen Salthouse was an angel because anything that needed doing, she did, including using a trap to catch a mouse in the kitchen. We added new toilets with baby changing facilities. (Dad's joke: *We didn't have that before because we had to keep the babies we'd got!*)

A pastor who had 'preached with a view' was having dinner with Anne and I. He asked, 'Do you think I'm right for the job? I said, 'I have some reservations.' He said, 'If I have to continue where I am for another year then I will do it to gain more experience.' He was working at a church where he was only being paid his expenses. I thought his attitude was very good and that he might make a pastor with some clear guidance. His preaching wasn't the best, but that could improve in time. He came to Great Eccleston. I helped him to plan a week out efficiently following the guidance I'd been given by my son, Pastor

Andrew (Fulwood Free Methodist Church). I explained that he needed to be flexible within this plan. I checked his progress and plan each week. For example, I told him to be in the church office from 8 – 12am so the people could easily contact him. He could also do his preparation at that time. However, after I left and no longer micro-managed him things soon changed and he returned to work from home and, sadly, things began to fall apart.

Lancaster

2000 – 2002: Lay Pastor in Lancaster

Allan Ellershaw asked me if I'd be interested in pastoring Lancaster. Barrie Walton and my brother Peter, for reasons that I couldn't understand, said they didn't think Anne was well enough to go to Lancaster. I prayed about it and then said, 'If it is right for us to go, the prompt needs to come from Anne herself.' Some weeks later, Anne and I were in an anniversary service at Lancaster when Anne put her hand on my knee and said, 'Have you ever thought about Lancaster again?' I smiled and said, 'I was waiting for you.' She said, 'The answer is yes.' Allan was there and I went straightaway and told him.

When I attended the introductory board meeting at Lancaster, I was wondering, 'What am I going to do and what vision can I give them?' which was somewhat unspiritual of me! But it turned out there was no need for me to speak at all because the ten members said, 'We have a building to build, but spiritually we feel flat and dead.' I said, 'Right. Let's get building in every way.' We will build the church practically and spiritually, and then the building at the back, which we eventually named Stepping Stones, which is the name suggested by Val Kilbride, because that was what the building was intended to be. Val was my secretary and we got on very well. She put me right when I was wrong, which of course wasn't very often (!) I called her "Bubbles" and still do today, because when I met her, her hair was all curls. She was also a bubbly personality who regularly opened services and welcomed everyone with cheerful enthusiasm. We got cracking with the building. There was a huge tree in the car park, but we weren't allowed to shift it because the neighbours like it. (2016: The tree was finally removed with permission because the roots were undermining the building.)

Roy Bourner came for an interview. He'd trained with World Evangelism Crusade who taught a brilliant work ethic. We wanted Roy for an evangelist because the leaders wanted someone to lead outreach. Several months later, Roy complained about some activities that weren't going quite the way he wanted. I said, 'You are the most miserable pastor I've ever met. You came here with £41,000 in the church bank, we've pointed the building to stop damp, we have painted inside and out, we put new carpets down, and there is a new building at the back. We have tarmacked the car-park, and provided you with the minibus you requested to bus children into church. Lots of pastors would have loved to come into such a healthy situation and simply got on with the job.

Anne never wanted to leave Lancaster because she'd made friends there, and was happy. However, I needed to go back to my home church and Roy needed to pastor without my overseeing.

Great Eccleston Again

2013 I became bothered that we were losing the Free Methodist identity. Some things were done with the best intentions but seemed, to my mind at least, rather sloppy. In my home church of Garstang, I could not have wished for more loving pastors in John Sainsbury and Marcie Potts, but I felt edgy. I also felt that perhaps, like the eagle in the eerie, when it is time for the eaglets to move on, the eagle (new pastor) disturbs the nest forcing the youngsters (in this case, me) to fly to pastures new, so I attended Fulwood for a few Sundays. I enjoyed the worship and the preaching immensely. I would have continued going there, but I'd had trouble with the pastor since the very day he was born! Occasionally, I also attended Great Eccleston.

One Sunday morning, I'd worshiped at Great Eccleston. Then the following week they held a memorial service for Peter Horrocks which I went to. There the pastor's wife, Sue Kelsall, said to me, 'I just want to tell you David, that when I saw you at Great Eccleston last Sunday morning, I thought how good it would be if you could come and get alongside us at Great Eccleston.' I had spoken on the Armour of God over three afternoon services at Fulwood FMC and later discovered that the pastoral worker, Sue Chastney, had recommended these talks to Pastor Chris and Sue Kelsall in Great Eccleston. I was asked to repeat the series there and this affirmed my decision to join that congregation.

I'd always got on well with Pastor Marcie from Garstang so I emailed her, quoting my Yorkshire mother-in-law's oft repeated phrase, 'It is as it is, if it isn't as it should be!' For me, at Garstang, I have to say it is as it is, if it isn't as David Gardner wants it to be. And rather than causing any ill-feeling I preferred to move on, so Garstang could find their way forward as pastors and leaders wanted, without me sticking my mot in.

Pastor Chris shared his vision with me for the church. He wanted to make the whole site into a place where people could come for seminars, weekends and so on. We would need to build new church premises and develop some of the land for sports activities, to make it accessible for the locals – a place to be used for outreach and community. When Chris shared his vision, an immediate thought came to me: 'Build it and they will come.' I know this is against all evangelistic practices and was actually inspired by the film 'Field of Dreams' but I see this development as the best way forward for Great Eccleston. The church building at present is the wrong shape. Sunday mornings it is almost full, which in church growth terms is too full.

Friendships

David and Liz Ollerton; Barrie and Eva Walton; Malcolm and Kaye Hartley; Alan and Marian Williamson; Terry and Jenny Tiddy

David and Liz Ollerton

Our friendship with David and Liz was lifelong. Anne and I had hoped to attend their wedding in Tunbridge Wells, but we stayed in Guildford with Mavis Marsh who had been Anne's bridesmaid. She gave us directions and the time it would take to drive to the venue, but South London was thick with traffic. We were too late and only made the reception.

David has always introduced me as his 'spiritual father' but if ever a son excelled his father spiritually, it is David. His grasp of scripture and church history is tremendous, and his love for people. His first pastoral appointment was in Old Kent Road with London City Mission. If he was preaching 'up north' David would stay with us, and with David in the house there was never a dull moment. All our kids dreaded him coming because he got up their noses, always challenging them as far as their faith was concerned. He has always been part of our home and we count him as a son.

Liz tells this anecdote: David refused to stop for the children on the motorway, saying, 'You have a potty, so use it.' Liz did let the kids use it - then she stuck the potty on David's lap as he was driving and said, 'Now you deal with it.'

Anne and I planned to stay at Loch Shin in the Central Highlands of Scotland. It happened that David and his son, Andrew, were going 'Munro-bagging' in the same area – meaning that they climb to the top of all the peaks in Scotland over 3000 feet. I'm sure that all this time spent going up Munros and talking with his father gave Andrew a good grasp of the Bible. They'd planned to live in tents, but because we had plenty of space in our bungalow, they moved in with us. They'd text us from the top of a Munro to say what time they'd be back for tea then they'd arrive later through the back door, via the boiler house, where they removed their wet gear, strewing it around the boiler to dry. David and Andrew thought this was great. Long after that holiday, David asked Anne, 'When are you going to Scotland again?' and she replied, 'I will never tell you that!' I was never sure how serious she was.

When I arrived in Cornwall to begin ministry I received a package in the post containing books about Billy Bray and The Bible Christians and Wesleyanism in Cornwall, with a note telling me, *This is so you will know what you are doing!'* It was, of course, from 'Olly' as we called him.

Anne and I visited the Ollertons in London, just after we had come out of Methodism. Olly and Mavis Towers had both applied to go to the mission field with Free Methodism, but one of the things listed on the form they had to complete was that they must not speak in tongues or encourage anyone else to do this. Pastor Frank Mitchell who moved in the things of the spirit as far as holiness was concerned, wrote an epistle to the bishops in the USA saying they were wrong to teach this. The bishops said that the UK could decide themselves who could go out onto the mission field. In the end, neither Olly nor Mavis went. David eventually applied to go to Bridgend Pentecostal Church in South Wales. Pastor Barrie Walton and myself went to his induction. After his interview with this Pentecostal church he was told by one of the senior elders, 'One thing is certain - you haven't come here to please *us* today. You have the job.' They did something that I thought was excellent, because in those days our pastors were underpaid - they paid Olly the average wage of the congregation. Olly and Liz had a flat. In the eaves Olly had a train set and a model layout of Green Ayre Station in Lancaster which is now gone. After a time, Olly moved to Esher in Surrey. Anne and I went to stay. One evening in their church, this lassie gave her testimony. David told me, 'Her family are Bentalls - millionaires who own a great department store with a bridge connecting two sides of the road.' Anne and I visited this store and to my great surprise, at the top of the stairs there was a man playing a grand piano. Wow! I have always valued our friendship and since Anne passed on, David keeps in touch, frequently ringing and checking up on me.

Barrie and Eva Walton

Back in the early 70s, I remember Barrie in the old wooden hut at Cabus Village Hall. There was a hole in the floor at one end of the hut. My parents both wanted to be baptised so Barrie got a bowl of water from the kitchen and baptised them by tipping water over their heads. Back then, Barrie was more of a pastor to us than a personal friend. He patiently put up with me because I was very much an emotional yo-yo, on the mountain top one week, and down the valley the next, like a spiritual roller-coaster.

As we formed the new Free Methodist movement in the UK, Barrie and I drew closer as friends. In my retirement (remember I was only 58 when I retired) Barrie encouraged me to lead churches but I never felt good enough to be a pastor. Forgetting about the forgiveness of God, I said, 'Sorry, I can't do this. In my own heart there are things that make me unfit to be a pastor.' Barrie approached me in spring 1990 and asked me to go to Cornwall throughout March April and May, to cover whilst Ken Leech was away in the USA.

One morning, while Ken Leech was praying, the name 'David Gardner' had come to him. Ken and I didn't know each other, but Ken told Barrie. Barrie told me about this, so I prayed, 'Lord, this is the second time of asking and you know me - so I can't refuse.' Anne and I went to Cornwall for those months. The following November Barrie requested I go again but as I have already related, this time he asked me to consider going for two years. Barrie was always supportive. I gained much confidence from his invitation. When my time in Cornwall was over, most likely at Barrie's prompting, the conference secretary Alan Ramm wrote to thank me. It had been the first conference experiment to put a lay preacher in place of full-time pastor.

Barrie and Eva and Anne and I occasionally holidayed together. Once we spent a few days in Marazion. I remember I had a bad back and ended up in Penzance getting physiotherapy. All of us called in to see Willie Rodda, of clotted cream fame, who was an elder at Scorrier Methodist Church near Redruth. Barrie had met him before at the revival meetings at Southport. As we were leaving Barrie spoke through the open car window, 'God bless you, Willie,' to which Willie replied, 'He does when I let him!' And I have used this story to illustrate our responsibility in being open to what God has for us.

I have always gone to Barrie and Eva for spiritual advice, with my questions and problems, and it has been really good. Eva once said to me, 'David, the Lord can use you - he once used an ass!' (Referring to Balaam's Ass in the Bible, Numbers 22 if you want to find it for yourself.) Since that time Eva has apologised a hundred times for saying it, but she was right and we still laugh about it. Eva set me an example when she prayed. She'd say, 'Lord I'm coming as sincerely as I can at this time.' This reminds me of the verse, *'Tis easy when with simple eye, thy loveliness we see, to consecrate ourselves afresh, to duty and to thee.'*

Over the last six years (2010-2016) the Waltons and I have become closer friends. Whenever we meet we discuss many things. We happily disagree or have a laugh. Now Jean (my lovely new wife) accompanies me when we visit.

I learnt many things from my friend Barrie, but here is one example: Barrie was an inspiring preacher – we'd discuss theological positions such as Calvinism or Arminianism. Barrie always said, 'Keep truths in tension, then you don't go down one particular lane and finish up in a cul-de-sac.'

I led a baptism service in the building belonging to the Apostolic Church in Porthleven and afterwards the pastor asked me, 'What are you?' I said, 'I'm a Calvinistic Armenian Pentecostal converted in a Methodist Church, baptised in a Baptist Church in Edinburgh and now I'm in Free Methodism.' He said, 'Oh,' and turned and walked away from me. Well, it was true. And I think most or all of my sons would come into that bracket! (That answer was inspired by Barrie's saying, 'Keep your truths in tension.')

Alan and Marian Williamson

I mentioned meeting Alan in my army days. Thus began a long and special friendship. Alan played the organ at our wedding in 1954 when I was 22 and Anne was 21. Alan trained to be a vet. He married Marian, a physiotherapist. They lived in Kendal and then moved to Blackburn, had four children, (now adults) and have lived in the same huge house ever since. We used to meet up on a regular basis. They have been very faithful friends and kept the friendship going even when I was careless about it. It wasn't Anne's fault as she was good at keeping up with people. I remember our two families going down Dolphinholme Church drive to go climbing styles and a walk through the Mill Woods, with all our children dressed in their Sunday best.

Malcolm and Kaye Hartley

Back in the 70s, Anne met Kaye through the Lydia prayer group. All four of us became friends. When we lived at Rivendell Mal and Kaye would come swimming each Friday night, and alternate Fridays we would make a meal for each other. We went on holidays to Spain and France together, the friendship remaining strong until Anne passed on. Mal always loved walking, orienteering and cycling, often with his son Gavin, until Gavin began to leave him behind! Their daughter Jacquie remains firm friends with our family.

Terry and Jenny Tiddy

Terry and Jenny live in Porthleven in Cornwall. For 23 years after leaving Helston we'd phone Terry and Jen every Sunday night and greet each other with the words of a Methodist hymn, 'And are we yet alive, each other's face to see?' We'd chat about Cornwall and family. They had holidays with us, including one when they enjoyed their 25th wedding anniversary at St Laurent's de Combes, our beautiful house in France. Terry (who used to be a postman) is a stolid person, completely reliable and Jen is Jenny, loving and cheerful. We have many laughs together. I'd call Jenny's mother, Miriam Watters, 'my second mum' because I lived with the Tiddys for a month after John and Caroline Townley moved into the manse in Helston. (John took over the pastoral role from me that September).

Scotland – Highlands and Low Points

2001: Anne and I embarked on a Hebridean Princess Cruise. We love Scotland and thought it would be nice do this, but it wasn't our scene what with drinks before *this and that* and having to dress up for dinner. I only had one suit. At night the covers were turned down and pyjamas were put out for us. We agreed it was a good experience of luxury at its best. On Islay, we visited the whisky factory. The whisky looked like iodine and tasted like iodine and smelt like iodine. It was terrible! One morning aboard the cruise ship at 11am, they provided a BBQ with marvellous food. Unfortunately, at 1pm they served up a three course lunch which was far too much for us. Classy? Not.

At night wherever we docked, we were entertained by local groups; singers, accordion players and dancers. It was lovely. One evening we were diverted to Mull because the swell was too heavy to land on one of the planned islands, so we were given a coach ride and trip around a castle.

2002: Anne and I bought a caravan and a Merc in which we set off to Mull. We'd been told by Mervyn France (who often goes to Mull) about a parking site on the other side of Tobermory with a lovely sandy beach. Ideal! We arrived to find a very ancient sign that read, *'No parking on the foreshore or staying overnight.'* Mervyn had obviously ignored this, but we daren't risk it. As it was impossible to do a U-turn with the caravan, we had to drive (at speed) all the way around Mull until we arrived back at the port where the official caravan site was. So we weren't so thrilled with Mull and I have never been back.

We planned another holiday in Scotland not realising this would be our last one together. I think Anne went for my sake, because she was already on crutches, suffering from osteoporosis. She had broken her femur in Lancaster church where there is a slight slope up. She really wasn't well. I should have had the sense to turn back at Hamilton services. As we were coming back from the restaurant through the services, the shop girl saw us and said, 'Just a minute, I'll get you a wheelchair.' We arrived at The Mains of Tay at Kenmore, The Stables, and found there were stairs. When we booked, we'd asked if there were any steps and they'd said no, but the bedrooms were upstairs. The owners let us use a large place holding 8 people as it had a downstairs ensuite. As we moved into it, Anne stepped down a step on crutches and fell, saying 'I've broken my leg again.' The medics arrived rapidly and took her to Perth A&E in an ambulance. There we learnt that she had broken both femurs. I stayed one night in a B&B near the hospital, on Glasgow Road. The rest of the week I travelled back to Kenmore to stay in our holiday place. Each day I drove the forty minutes to the hospital and stayed until 9pm before going back. Jason kindly drove up from Harrow. The Kenmore people let him stay with me and gave him an airbed. I woke one morning thinking Jason had gone for a walk, the next thing he appeared dripping wet at the French doors. He'd been in the hot tub in the garden. The next week, after Kenmore, David had booked me in at a cottage in Fife, 7 miles from the hospital.

Eventually Anne came to Lancaster Royal by ambulance. She stayed there 13 weeks. They pinned her right leg, which was fine, but her left leg already had a pin in and they couldn't do anything but splint the leg. She had to use crutches and eventually a wheelchair. Anne never really recovered. The osteoporosis was getting more of a grip and she became frailer.

We were living at Gillows Green. I'd been nursing Anne for a couple of years, unable to leave her and being on duty 24/7. Very occasionally we'd go out, maybe to Barton Grange, where I could wheel her round in her wheelchair which was very dangerous for our finances as there was a lot of stuff at wheelchair height which she could reach! She'd pop things into the basket she carried on her knees but it lifted her spirits. At this time I was not aware that I was being drained, but the rest of my family had noticed and had had some discussion between them about how best to support us. In the January of 2012 one Tuesday afternoon, David and Jayne, carrying towels and bedding, walked into the kitchen and said, 'Dad, we are coming to look after you and mum.' They committed themselves to whatever nursing care was going to be needed. With this in mind, we proceeded to convert the garage into a lounge for Anne and I. It had double doors for wheelchair access and a door through to our bedroom with ensuite bathroom.

David and Jayne were not to know that within two months, on March 3rd, Anne would be with the Lord. About a month earlier, unbeknown to me, Dr Miles and Sister Helen with David and Jayne had set up palliative care. I remember Anne lying in bed saying to Dr Miles (crouched on his haunches talking to her) 'Am I going to die?' Dr Miles said, 'Yes.' Anne never batted an eyelid; she knew her eternity was secure.

I had mixed feelings at this point. On the one hand I was relieved for Anne, knowing her destiny was secure in Christ, and was no longer daily saying 'David, you have no idea how this pain is,' despite the fact she was on morphine. Also, after knowing each other for sixty-seven years and the loving relationship we had developed, there was what I can only describe as *a tremendous gap within me*.

It was tough to even consider a funeral. Anne had been rushed into hospital the Monday previous to the Saturday on which she had died, against the thoughts of Dr Miles that he would never return her to hospital. He had hoped to allow her to pass away at home. Nevertheless, he had had to send her in. David Jnr and I were allowed to stand by her head while three doctors were trying to resuscitate her, and the registrar took us into a side room and told us there probably wasn't much chance of her making it. However, Anne pulled through and came home. She died on the Saturday. Dr Miles had not attended her during the remaining days at home (after this time in hospital), so he came to apologise because he couldn't legally sign off the death certificate. Anne's body had to go back to Lancaster for a specialist who had last seen her to sign her off. This delayed the funeral.

Our family all gathered together. The funeral was arranged. We anticipated high numbers so we decided to use Fulwood Free Methodist church for the service. I attended wearing a sport's jacket, bright tie and shirt because the Sunday before Anne died she had told me what to put on – as she had always done, so everything matched all right!

We'd always wanted David Ollerton to take our funerals. He picked up something that had happened, that at the four different churches I had been involved in, it had never been 'David is at. . .' but 'David and Anne are at. . .' And he was right. I hadn't realised how much Anne had been involved until I read the condolence cards, many containing thanks to Anne for prayer and counselling.

The funeral achieved what we wanted as a commemoration while giving glory to God for all that had happened in our lives and for our loving family. Charis composed a song for Anne only the day before, which was beautiful. The service had such an impact, our solicitor David Bennetts was present. Afterwards he came to me and said he had never been in a service like it in his life. This was because God was so present in the service.

Our grand-daughter Charis Smith was inspired to write a beautiful song and set it to piano. Her brother-in-law, Mark Shotter, kindly offered to learn the tune on the morning of the funeral. He played so sensitively as Charis sung during the service in Fulwood Free Methodist church.

There's something bitter sweet about you leaving us tonight
I know that you were ready for this time
But many people stay behind and long for you to be
Still here, still breathing, still be

Oh it's painfully painful to have loss in your life
Being sorry doesn't seem to fill the space
But it's beautifully lovely how God welcomes you in
His timing is perfect; it's bitter, yet it's sweet

There was a different kind of peace left
In the room when you were gone
A lingering of perfume in the air
A humbling reality that in us you will still be here,
And I thank my Father God for all He did in your life
You displayed the love that He gives
And I cannot help but praise God for the family you grew
Grounded in faith, hope and truth

Oh it's painfully painful to have loss in your life
Being sorry doesn't seem to fill the space
But it's beautifully lovely how God welcomes you in
His timing is perfect; it's bitter, yet it's sweet

In the days that followed I felt very down and at a loss and lonely, even though I was very aware of God's presence. It was evident to my family I was getting

162

nowhere. I bumbled about doing nothing (maybe pottered in the garden a bit). I'd get up, have a quiet time and fix my own breakfast. I'd look for Vinny to accompany me as I fed the hens. Every evening David and Jayne would call, 'Dad, dinner's ready' and I'd go through to the kitchen to eat with them. I spent the rest of the evening in my room and then go to bed. Once a week I'd head to Preston for a few hours to work on this book with Katharine; sometimes I'd do a pastoral visit or maybe a hospital visit.

Someone had suggested I wrote a letter to Anne to express how I was feeling. I did this but after two sessions it wasn't helping my emotions, and by Christmas 2012 I stopped. Later, I was talking with David and Liz Ollerton, answering their questions about my life. After me rattling on for half an hour they said, 'David you ought to get this written down for the sake of your grandchildren.' So I started writing, not letters to Anne, but my memories. I made very little progress. Katharine looked at my efforts and said, 'You've only written one side! Why don't we meet each week and you can talk while I type?' And so this 'talking' has continued week on week, except for a big break because something wonderful happened to cheer me up. But for that story you must read the final chapter.

'Things I Have Learnt'
'The Main Thing'

'I Now Realise' is the title of a sermon I once preached, based on the words of Peter in Acts 10 verse 34: Peter said, *'I now realise God is no respecter of persons.'* The main

thrust is to allow the Holy Spirit to speak into your heart so you realise you need to move on. It is a fantastic passage, so important that the gospel writer Luke repeated the whole thing in chapter 11. This is about the Gentiles receiving the Holy Spirit, but Peter was so hung up on Judaism, that not only him, but all the disciples back then, even though they'd been filled with the Spirit and experienced a marvellous day (called Pentecost), these men still needed to realise that there was *more*.

Dierdre Brower Latz, the Principal of the Nazarene College, preached at Garstang on Acts 10. She talked about Cornelius and Peter, but if you look at the story, *the main thing* is the conversion of the Gentiles as well as the *everyday story of walking with the Holy Spirit,* both for Cornelius and Peter. God is pouring his Spirit on the Gentiles, so who are they to moan about that? I spoke to Dierdre about her sermon. I told her that in 1950 I'd heard Maynard James, a great Nazarene preacher, who said, *'My heart is aching.'* I was thinking of the Geoffrey Brothers who brought Pentecostalism to the UK and that we didn't like some of the things they did because we considered them to be a bit 'way out,' but they did bring to the fore the Person of the Holy Spirit. Our churches must not die from the hardening of the arteries because we don't recognise fully the work of the Holy Spirit.

By this I mean that the Holy Spirit gives us *freedom.* In my spiritual life my sons taught me about being at ease with God, (meaning to be free, but not easy, with God). As a father I'm sorry I made Sunday a *don't* day and not a *do* day. I went about it legalistically instead of in the freedom that Christ gives. [Andrew says: 'Dad once told me that he prayed for me personally that I'd know liberty but not licence in life.' I believe Dad's prayer has been answered because I struggle with any form of legalism and I tell others that my highest value is freedom.']

Being a Carer

My relationship with God has certainly deepened through the past three challenging years. I now understand how much it takes out of carers, not just physically, but mentally and spiritually, when they are worried about the person they love twenty-four-seven.

Modern Songs

I can be pretty opinionated about the words we sing in church. For example, we might be singing something like 'Here I stand broken-hearted' but it seems to me there are no broken-hearted people in the room, although that is only my opinion. Most likely I can't tell what's going on inside those around me. All the same, for me, the words we sing ought to have meaning in reality. Many modern songs appear to turn our attention onto ourselves and they don't focus on Christ. David Ollerton sent me a disc containing 13 songs but he said there is only one good one on it; 'The Power of the Cross.' It is relatively modern and very good. The Wesleys wrote thousands of hymns. Back in their day, folk must have said, 'Not another hymn by Charles or John!' What amazes me is that when we do sing most hymns the worship is strong because the singing is more rhythmic. We older generation struggle to keep up with some of the modern stuff. (In my opinion many of the words are not nearly as good - but maybe this will change as new songs are created.)

Hymns and What Inspires Me

I love songs and music by Charis, especially the one she wrote in response to her accident (she was hit by a car in November 2006) and wrote that special song 'O Lord I Cry to Thee.' Then, as mentioned just before her grandmother's funeral, Charis composed a beautiful tribute song called 'Anne's Song' that I listened to many times in my car.

Hymns play great part in my life. I miss them so much. Over the years I learnt so much theology from hymns. I like 'And Can It Be' - a very progressive hymn that begins with the idea of how can I get this 'God-life' when I'm such a mess? It ends with 'no condemnation'. When I take Barrie and Eva out in the car we play hymns and we are blessed. Many words have meant so much to me during difficult times. One such goes: *'Here in this maddening maze of things . . . I know that God is good.'* Or, *'My heart so low be laid, but God is round about me, I cannot be dismayed.'*

Prayer

I've often prayed, 'Lord keep me real,' because I am very good at going through the motions of being Christian. I'm like the well-known author Eugene Petersen who writes how he can feel 'thick and dull,' then suddenly God breaks in and clarity strikes once more.

I never pray help my unbelief, because my unbelief doesn't need any help. This is a saying I agree with. Doubt and uncertainty are part and parcel of being human. Nevertheless, I look forward to prayer meetings. Not everyone is clear how to lead others in prayer; it is a gift to do this well. We can develop bad habits in public prayer. For example, some always start with the words 'Lord we just -' or use a kind of evangelical vocabulary uncommon to everyday folk. Silence may be a good thing at the right time, but sometimes there are such long silences that it can be uncomfortable and not necessarily about God's presence. We all need encouragement to pray because we have a tendency to think our own ideas or prayers are insignificant. Not everyone is like Wesley who would rise early to spend 2-3 hours praying. We must be ourselves before God. I used to say to the group, 'Let's each of us say just one thing we are thankful for.' Sidlow Baxter used to say, 'No prayer is ever too small.' Everyone and anyone can pray. Something written around the time of the First World War went, 'Why are you afraid of such a thing like praying out loud when there are young men going to die in trenches?' I used to start off my prayer times by saying 'Lord I am coming to you . . .' but later I questioned myself, and my approach. 'What am I saying that for? I am already *there,* in God's presence!'

One of the most inspiring books I've ever read is 'Reversed Thunder' by Eugene Peterson. He says if God always did what *we* think he should do, he'd have to keep meddling in human affairs and we'd experience no freedom, no free choice. Before I read Reversed Thunder I used to pray for what I thought my family needed, but now I mention each one by name ('Each one' meaning, all my adult children and their families.) I simply say to God, 'They are all yours. Your will be done.' So I'm no longer asking God to meddle in our lives.

Hitchhikers

I used to pick up hitchhikers whenever I saw them but nowadays I don't dare stop. Once, I offered a lift to a smartly dressed hitchhiker, who told me he was a shop steward in Leyland. This man said, 'We go in to our bosses to demand extra money or time off and they're so keen to rush out to the golf courses that they give in more quickly than they used to.' He sounded triumphant as he said, 'There's no one can stop us now, is there?'

Another time, the famous Brash Bonsall, (the then principal of Birmingham Bible Institute, 'BBI,' where 12 of our young church folk were studying) was coming to preach at Dolphinholme Chapel. When Brash came he would stay in our home - we were impressed that he always read his Greek Bible! Anyway, as I was driving through Lancaster I saw a man in a bowler hat walking briskly along so I stopped to offer him a lift. He was about to walk the full seven miles from Lancaster train station to our house in Dolphinholme. Yes, it was Brash!

Brash brought an audio tape with him about BBI which he wanted me to play. Back then, tape recorders were rare. I borrowed a Grundig Four Track Player from Uncle Joe Towers. Try as I may I could not get this tape to work. After twenty minutes I suddenly pressed another button and it worked. Brash said, 'I was just praying the Lord would help me sort this problem out.' He told me a story of being ill in bed, in Canada. He said, 'The Lord laid on my heart some Chinese who were in a harbour and I prayed fervently for whoever they were. I had no idea where or what it meant. So I prayed and later found out that there'd been a revival in that town among the Chinese people.' Barrie and I went to BBI to visit our 12 people there, Phil and Audrey Talbot and Allan and Sue Ellershaw, Dave Ollerton and Sheila Etherington and Mavis Towers and others. The students made lunch. Their very own home-made cabbage soup. It was dreadful – dreadful.

The Third Age (or Being Somewhat Older)

Old age is a privilege but it obviously brings its difficulties. I am blessed with generally good health, although my energy is waning.

I have something floating in my right eye. If it gets worse I will have to get it seen to. When I first saw it I thought, 'Ugh! A blimmin' fly,' and I was trying to catch it until I realised it was a bit of light and so I gave in trying to catch it. It is something in the gelatinous fluid in my eyes. Nothing to worry about. We are fearfully and wonderfully made.

On Daughter-in-Laws and Arthur

It goes without saying that all my children married extremely good-looking, talented people! How did they do it I wonder? We certainly raised up a fine brood! Our six daughters-in-law and Arthur all have a keen sense of humour, a love of justice and show great care for those in need.

Timothy married Sheila Woodhouse in 1977. It was amazing for Anne and I to think that our oldest son was married already. At time of writing, they still live in our beloved Dolphinholme with their much adored standard poodle Mitch. For years Timothy and Sheila were strongly involved with Kays Farm Fellowship. Sheila is a musician, plays the piano and sings beautifully, often in churches. They have had some international adventures such as visiting church groups in Iceland and India.

It was my brother Peter who told me he had just had a meal out with 'Andrew's future wife.' This meal happened several months before they got engaged. Peter had met up with Andrew and Katharine in London in 1979 as he was passing through. He'd treated them to a Chinese meal and, although it was early days, he'd sussed out the relationship. Andrew met Katharine at The London School of Theology. 1981 they married in Emmanuel Church, Northwood. Katharine's uncle Martin officiated and I was asked to say prayers in the service. Katharine trained as a teacher. They worked at Yeldall Manor, a drug and alcohol rehab, before moving to Preston in 1984 for Andrew to be the first assistant pastor in the Free Methodist Church in the UK. Their daughters Susanna, Kirsty-Jane and Charis are all married.

Three months after Andrew and Katharine's wedding in 1981, our lovely daughter Cherith got married to Arthur Lodge in Garstang Free Methodist Church. Cherith was a nurse and Arthur a lithographic printer in Leicester. Their children, Matthew and Daniel and Hannah-Rose have grown up to be hard-working, good people. At the time of writing, Hannah is engaged to Jon Grant, a Baptist pastor. Their wedding will be 11th March 2017.

David married Jayne Gibson – the daughter of a local livestock haulage family. After Anne passed away, David and Jayne moved permanently into Gillows Green which was a wonderful support to me. Their oldest daughter Alex is married to Philip Sayer who had grown up through Garstang Free Methodist Church. Alex and Phil presently attend Lancaster Free Methodist Church with their toddler son Zeb.

Simon married Julie Bailey. They had been going out since the age of 14. Simon has worked not only for Safegard Storage, but also as a Free Methodist Pastor in Lancashire and Cornwall. Julie is a first class administrator and a great mum to Zak, Joel and Maria. Julie's family hail from the other side of the border, Yorkshire!

Jonathon married Sarah Gibbons, a local girl who was brought up attending Garstang Free Methodist Church. For many years she has cheerfully worked in The Christian Resource Centre in Preston. Jonny has also worked both for our business and in the church. He now works as a driver. Their sons Luke, Adam and Joe are a credit to them.

Jason married Rachel Earwicker. They live in Harrow, London with their daughter Daisy. Jason has recently trained for the Anglican ministry, while Rachel continues her work as a speaker, writer and leader who inspires young people, especially girls, to be strong and cope in today's modern sexualised society.

Peter (my brother) and his wife Marian's daughter are parents to Katie and Philip. Katie is married to David (The name David means *beloved* or *friend,* so maybe that explains why there are so many of us!) Katie worked as a valued administrator for the family company, but since has worked in the Christian Resource Centre for many years. Their children are Joanna and Nathan. Philip lives in Australia with his wife Robyn and their children William, Marguerite and Yvette.

Katie Gardner marries David Devany at
Garstang Free Methodist Church, posing beside the
beautiful red Winmarleigh Schooner

15th February 1995 From the Lancaster Guardian

Lancaster based haulier, Safegard Storage, is hoping for another long-term partnership that matches the on-going 20-year relationship it has enjoyed with MAN. This time between Managing Director Pete Gardner's daughter, Katie, and her husband David Devany. The happy couple were recently married at the Garstang Free Methodist Church with a special guest – an MAN 22.422FVLT twin steer tractor acting as the wedding 'truck'. Driver-of-honour was Mr. Gardner's nephew and Transport Manager, David Gardner Jr., who needed all his driving skills to reverse into the 9ft 2in wide church gates (No doubt MAN's superb manoeuvrability helped!) Congratulations to Katie and David and best wishes for the future.

Childhood Accidents

Amazing examples of what our offspring survived

Timothy and the Fire

This happened on the Saturday night that baby Jason came home from hospital. Someone knocked on our door yelling, 'You've got a fire!' Earlier that day, Tim had been burning rubbish at the end of one of the buildings and, as far as we knew the fire was out, but it must have gone under the sawdust, creeping until it got to one of the wooden buildings. I reacted quickly, moving a lorry in such a hurry that I snapped the air-pipes and electrics because it wasn't coupled up properly. We managed to move two vehicles out of the burning building – but maybe we should have left one of them in because it was worth nothing and we could have got the insurance.

Timothy and the Nappy - and the Fire

As a toddler, Timothy dragged a Terry nappy through an open fire, and across the floor to the settee - or so I'm told.

Andrew and the Drain

Aged 2, Andrew had been playing outside near a drain. He put a washer from the drain into his mouth. Within 2 hours he'd gone from being a healthy happy child, to being in hospital, seriously ill with some nasty bug. He could have died.

Andrew and the Bomb

Andrew was about 14 years old. His friend from the Free Methodist Church, Thomas Parkinson, and Andrew used to argue about whether or not they played on the family farm in Catforth or came to our house to go out riding in one of the cattle trucks. That day they went to Tom's farm. For some reason they knew you could make small bombs using domestic products and gardening chemicals. They experimented using cut off sections of an old exhaust pipe. They ingeniously drilled a hole through it to make a wick of string soaked in petrol. They finally made several bombs with which they blew up concrete-sized breeze blocks into gravel-sized chunks. They decided to make another one twice the size. They were inside an old hen hut (12x8ft). It was like a garden shed. They'd packed the bomb with the chemicals and Tom was finishing it off by, um, hammering down one end of it, when it exploded. Tom felt the main force of the blast. Both the lads blew across the shed. As Tom had been holding the bomb it blew off his thumb and the tops of two fingers.

Tom went to hospital. Andrew was mostly okay, but for some minor chemical burns on his face and his ears ringing for a day or two afterwards. The amazing thing was that when Andrew returned to see the shed after Tom had gone to hospital, just to look, he found the remains of the bomb and realised that only half of it had gone off. Tom could have been killed if the whole thing had gone off. The next day Andrew wandered back in and found the top of Tom's thumb. He didn't know what to do with it so he flushed it, like a dead goldfish, down the toilet. By then Tom had already had operations on his hands so the thumb would have been useless anyway. No one told the boys off. The police may have been involved but I can't remember. In hospital the nurses nicknamed Tom "our little IRA man!" because it was the early 1970s. Can you imagine how much media reaction there would be today?

Cherith and the Pram

When Simon was a baby, seven-year-old Cherith took him for a walk in the pram. She took him down Four Lane Ends past Tim and Sheila's and on. Local man, Septimus Brindle, had inscribed '30 years of Good Driving' on the front of his car. We reckoned it was 30 years of folk managing not to hit his car. Septimus Brindle's car hit the pram. Cherith remembers her shoes being found over the other side of a wall. She hurt her legs and spent a few days in bed but didn't need to go to hospital. It was obviously frightening for her. Peter and I took Simon to the hospital. His head was huge. It was touch and go for ten days. After a few days his head was still swollen. Medics gave him several transfusions to help relieve all the fluid in his head. What a joy when he recovered and returned home safe and well.

The Lord must have had his hands on Simon's life because as a teenager he was in a rally car that went off the road into a fence and a fence post went over his left shoulder narrowly missing him. He could have been dead twice.

David and the Fork Truck

David had only been employed by the firm for one month when, at the end of July, he rolled the forklift over. With little experience, he'd been driving too fast (as David says, 'out of my brain!') and tore flat out down the hangar then turned a very sharp left The whole thing tipped forward, smashed his foot and knocked the end of his big toe clean off. If it had hit his head, he would not have survived. Andrew raced him to hospital where he received 22 stitches at the end of the toe. David says, 'Nowadays my big toe nail is so thick I have to use wire cutters to cut it!'

Simon and the Dog Tablets

Some of the children would stay in Wilpshire with our family friends the Williamsons who had four children. Alan was a vet. One time, Cherith had to take Simon with her. Alan had put some dog-tablets by the phone, waiting for a customer to collect. Simon ate some of them. (I bet he felt RUFF!) And once again, Simon survived something horrible. Then again, this story might have been about Jonny and no one can remember.

Jonny and the Rallies

Jonny was 19 or 20 when he went to Top Rank for petrol and put a can of the stuff in the back of his car. Half a mile away, the car caught fire because he'd left the can of petrol up against the battery which was still hot from doing rallying. The petrol caught fire from the friction between the metal tin. The whole car burnt out.

Jonny used to reccy for the car rallies – once, over Harris End – he'd walk miles then I'd have to go out to fetch him! Once he fell in the Dyke at Dunsop Bridge, and I got called to rescue him. He had walked right back to a farm at Marshaw, through the Trough of Bowland to ring me for help. (No mobiles in those days!)

Jason and um, Sunday School

Lads will be lads and Sunday school at Garstang Free Methodist could involve some rough and tumble. Little surprise then that sometimes it ended being more rough than tumble. One Sunday when Jason was seven years old, a lad who was particularly big for his age (that's Jason's excuse) gave him a big shove and he fell over, putting his arm out to stop his fall. That resulted in a greenstick fracture and a trip to A and E in Sharoe Green hospital in Preston. He returned with only a sling, and no cast. Jason says, 'When I went back for the check-up I had to squeeze a little Mickey Mouse somersault toy for them to gauge that my strength was returning!'

Safegard Accident – Evening Post, Friday Jan 20th 1995

FIREMEN FREE DRIVER AFTER LORRIES COLLIDE

A driver had to be cut free from his lorry by firemen after he was involved in an accident in Lancaster. The man is an employee of Parkinson's haulage firm. He was driving west along Ashton Road yesterday when he was in collision with another HGV, from the company Safegard, which was travelling in the same direction. Emergency crews, battling against high winds and driving sleet, were called at about 3pm. Firemen used cutting equipment to free one of the men from his cab. He was taken to Royal Lancaster Infirmary with injuries to his arm. The second man walked away without injury. The accident left one vehicle (Parkinsons) in the middle of the country road close to the Royal Albert Hospital and shunted another towards a garden hedge. Sgt David Turner of Lancaster police said, 'Both HGVs were travelling in the same direction so we do not yet know how the accident could have happened. Our accident investigation team will be looking into the accident.'

Our Children

Back row: Andrew, me, Cherith, Timothy
Left centre: David. Centre: Anne
Front: Simon, Jason, Jonathon

Over the following pages, I will tell you a little about each of my (now adult) children in turn. Whatever I say cannot possibly do justice to the measure of love, joy and friendship each of them have brought into my life. They and their families have been, and continue to be, a great blessing to me.

Timothy David - born September 14th 1955

Tim is such a friendly man. He knows so many people who love him and his wife, Sheila (nee Woodhouse). He is caring and thoughtful and very supportive of others. When Timothy was a baby he had bad eczema. Despite this he was a very placid baby. As he grew, his eczema developed into asthma. When he was a young boy, we were holidaying at Rumbling Bridge in Scotland and Tim had asthma. We took him to a doctor. He got his first inhaler.

In the early days, we owned The Stable Yard (originally a place for stabling horses), but we stored coal there among other things. Dick Winder rented part of it off us to use as a building yard, paying us a mere 7 shillings and 6 pence (less than 40p) per week. I had bought the Stable Yard off Dad and sold it to Roy Whiteside for £10,000. Roy converted The Stable Yard into houses and Timothy had the privilege of buying the very first of these, 1 Stable Yard, for only £18,000. He and Sheila have lived there ever since.

When he was young, Timothy used to cycle to work at Hollins Lane, Forton, to help my brother Peter with the ICI depot that was situated in the old threshing yard. Today this place is a housing estate called Threshers Court. He was a quiet, reliable youngster who enjoyed working.

He always loved driving. When he's not in his HGV he drives countless miles in his car just to visit people, or to attend a church event. There were only 3 of our men ever passed the class 1 HGV first time: me, Harold Baines and our Timothy!

Andrew Joseph - born November 10th 1956 at home in Portree.

Andrew studied theology in London, where he met Katharine Ann Angel. On August 1st 1981 they married in Emmanuel Church Northwood. Their three daughters, Susanna Clare 1st October 1984; Kirsty-Jane 25th April 1986; Charis Elizabeth 8th November 1988.

Andrew has fairness in his mind, but as a young man he could be impetuous like me. He was also the biggest rebel. We had a rule that when the children were in our house they had to go to church once a week, but he rebelled against this. I reminded him, 'You have had an experience of God,' and he said with some sarcasm, 'Have I, Dad?'

In the late 70s, we rented a hangar at Burscough aerodrome. Peter and I thought Andrew could manage it for us, so Anne and I drove to Loughborough to see Andrew, to ask him if he'd be interested in coming home to run the depot. He agreed, because university life wasn't suiting him at that time. So each day he drove our red van to work. If anyone asked the way to Burscough we'd say, 'Head for Preston and follow the red marks on the road all the way.' Andrew wasn't one for driving slowly.

I felt disappointed when Andrew completed his theology degree in London because, instead of returning to Lancashire, he went to work at Yeldall Manor, a drug and alcohol rehabilitation centre near Reading, but later I realised what a good foundation this experience was for his future ministry. In 1983 while Andrew and Katharine were living there, Anne and I took Simon, Jonny and Jason on a canal boat holiday on the Thames. We wanted to do something different and Anne thought it would be great to go on the water. So we set off from Abingdon to go to Thames Ditton. This trip was intended to take seven days, but much to Anne's disgust we completed the trip in three days. I may have pushed it a little! Anyway we saw Windsor Castle which was brilliant. On the Sunday we moored at Henley to look around. As we walked up the high street we bumped into Andrew and Katharine walking along eating an ice cream - on the Sabbath! They joined us on the boat for an hour or two but Katharine was very allergic and her eyes streamed with hay fever. We visited Thames Ditton and Hampton Court where we walked around the gardens. We also went to London Zoo. That night we had our first ever Chinese meal. The whole adventure was amazing.

Growing up, Andrew had tended to take the lead in the family and was very helpful with the babies. He was good in the home. Tim kind of followed Andrew – but that was their nature. We always called Andrew 'fiddle fingers' because he'd pick up everything and tinker with it, sometimes accidentally breaking things in the process. One night Tim actually saved his life because Andrew had hold of a broken lamp flex and was badly shocked. He could not let go – and amazingly Tim took the plug out of the wall.

[Note: the family photograph on the following page was added because it includes so many people mentioned in this book, including three of the five children belonging to Anne's brother, Joe]

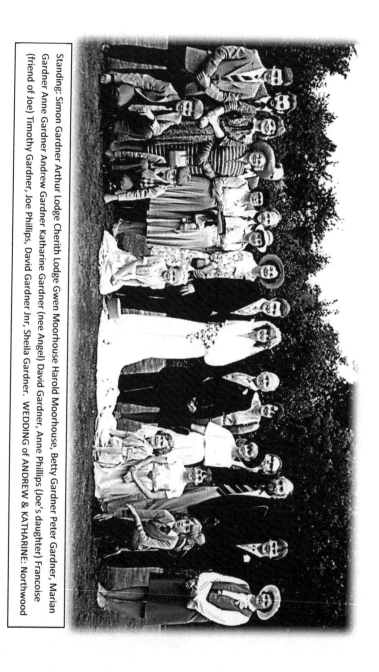

Standing: Simon Gardner Arthur Lodge Cherith Lodge Gwen Moorhouse Harold Moorhouse, Betty Gardner Peter Gardner, Marian Gardner Anne Gardner Andrew Gardner Katharine Gardner (nee Angel) David Gardner, Anne Phillips (Joe's daughter) Francoise (friend of Joe) Timothy Gardner, Joe Phillips, David Gardner Jnr, Sheila Gardner. WEDDING of ANDREW & KATHARINE: Northwood

Cherith Elizabeth - born 16th December 1958

Cherith married Arthur Lodge in November 1981 and lived in Leicester. Their children are Matthew, Daniel and Hannah-Rose.

Cherith has a kind and generous nature. She has the gift of wonderful friends and lovely people around her who love her. Once I tried to be honest with Cherith by sharing that I was feeling tired. But she said, 'No you are stressed out.' I said 'No, just tired.' I think I was somewhat impatient and the conversation finished on a bad note. As a young teenager Cherith left us to go nursing, eventually living in Leicester. When she comes to visit she likes to stay with Aunty Betty. They have a lifetime of care, love and mutual support. I was glad of Arthur's overseeing their finances but I did hope he'd stand up for Cherith when her sons teased her but he didn't seem to. He's a hard worker and a good dad. Their children are good, really amazing with good jobs and making lives for themselves. I felt very sad about the divorce.

David Whitaker – born 24th July 1961

For some reason young David went to stay with Anne's cousin Rita and her husband Bernard. They treated him so well that we joked that changed him for life! Everything he wanted he seemed to get. He came straight from school to work with us, despite both Anne and Peter being keen for the boys to go away for at least one year to do some maturing and get some life experience. However, we sent David to Livingston Technical College to train as a mechanic. He was only 16 years old, but off he went to college on a train with his leg in plaster! I don't think he's ever forgiven us.

One of the best things about David's mechanical knowledge was that Peter and I no longer had to bluff that we understood Geoffrey's fettling ways! David eventually became a transport manager. He could be late for work. To my mind, David was a marvellous preacher and worship leader. I remember hearing David communicating so clearly at the Great Eccleston church. He'd often preach from the aisle rather than the pulpit. On one occasion he used a mechanics illustration, as he held an ugly-looking metal thing – a trailer valve – explaining that the beautiful trailer was useless without it. I'd tell you the meaning but you can easily work it out for yourself.

Simon Peter – born 31st July 1965

Simon married a Yorkshire lass, Julie Bailey. When they got engaged, her dad Ken gave us a box of Yorkshire teabags - our War of the Roses! Their children are Zak, Joel and Maria. Simon is earnest, positive and honest in character. He's also very forthright – the boldest of my children to tell me where I go wrong! He's very much a middle child and may have struggled a little in the melee of the large family. Maybe he missed out on fully developing a relationship with his parents because he was born at a funny time in our business life. During his formative years, it wasn't us that were running the business but the business was running us. I was going out late at night to pick up the wagons so they'd be back and ready by morning. Simon did an apprenticeship as an auto-electrician for Ribblesdale

Electrics and at the end of the day he'd wait near the Tickled Trout in Salmesbury for us to pick him up. I used to wonder if he ever worried that we'd forgotten him as he waited alone under the bridge. Also he qualified as an electrician at night school in Blackburn. Simon eventually came to work for us as a fork-truck driver. He told us he wanted to go to Bible College, worked out his own finances and off he went. He was so good pastorally at Fulwood then Garstang that people still ask after him and miss his caring manner. When he preaches he speaks with great warmth and sincerity. A while back he took a step back from the ministry and I was worried for him but he said, 'God hasn't let me down in 17 years and he won't do that now.'

Simon trained as a driving instructor and gave me a free lesson. Before he qualified, John Townley asked him to help out in the Truro Church when the pastor Jonny Giddings became unwell. After an initial hesitation, Simon and Julie moved to Cornwall where he gave some more years to the ministry.

Christopher Paul
Born 3am October 6th 1966
Died 4.50pm November 17th 1966

Losing Christopher didn't impact me as much as Anne – I wouldn't allow her to go the funeral because it would have been too much for her. Christopher was born with heart problems and unable to thrive. He could not control his temperature. He was blue so we tried to keep him warm near the fire but then he got blisters. When we moved him a little away he quickly became cold again. Christopher had already been seen by a lovely doctor at Beaumont hospital, so in the middle of the night we took him there hoping to see the same man. However, a different doctor appeared and turned us away. We had no idea why he did this or what to do. We knew Doctor Reardon who lived at Whitewell in Forton, so we knocked on his door at three o'clock in the morning. Obviously he was in his pyjamas. He tried to help us, and Anne was that upset he gave her a glass of gin to calm her down. After drinking it, Anne wondered what on earth had happened to her!

When Christopher died we planted a tree in his memory. It is in the front garden of Portree, our family home in Dolphinholme. Not so long ago I discovered that Anne had written 'Christopher' and the date of his death in her Bible. Andrew remembers as a boy, singing Christopher to sleep in his pram.

Jonathon Mark – born 24th June 1968

Jonny was born in Lancaster Royal Infirmary; to my mind the least rebellious of all my children in that he didn't argue with us verbally (the way Andrew used to). Jonny came to work for us straight from school, although Anne would have preferred all the boys to work for others first, to gain experience. Jonny is a deep thinker and his loyalty and faithfulness are so positive. He didn't always communicate and tell us what was going on.

We had a rule that as long as the children were under our roof they went to church once on Sundays and he complied. When Jonny was 16 he and his friend Mark Mynett got into Heavy Metal. Anne used to iron his Iron Maiden clothes with her eyes shut tight! Mark played guitar at Jon's wedding and 'Here comes the bride!' squealed out like a cat being swung around by its tail! It wasn't the sort of music I understood, but I do know that he is highly talented!

It was a Tuesday morning. Jonny was 28. Princess Diana had been killed two days before. Jonny came into the kitchen and hugged his mum. He was crying. I thought he was pulling our leg because of Diana but Anne said, 'No, this is real. It's deeper than that.' Jonny told us he'd recommitted his life to Christ. He and Sarah became church members and dedicated all three of their sons at the same time. He said, 'I have so much catching up to do, I need to go to Bible College.' Of course we were thrilled.

Jon worked for us, and became our forklift instructor so he could test others and get them their CPC. He did pastoral work at Penwortham for a number of years. Presently he is enjoying driving trucks again. Pastoring and all things 'driving' seem to be the go-to work for our sons!

Jason Matthew – born 18th October 1971

Our youngest child Jason was born when we were living at the Hollies. His older brothers nicknamed him 'Mummy's Little Lamb!' As a child he was imaginative, enjoying playing with action men (hanging them from the bannisters) and messing about with his big brother Jonny.

As regards our business, Jason was excellent at repackaging goods such as Burton's Biscuits as well as a substitute milk powder for lambs. Jason would put on his headphones, and work hard on the line, often completing the best output per hour. A theologian friend of Jason's, Mark Greene, once wrote to tell us that Jason had a 'razor-sharp mind.' Jason had done some writing on 'futuristic' stuff and Mark was offering him work with LICC (London Institute of Contemporary Christianity). When Jason was at university I thought he might be messing about a bit so I asked him, 'How are you getting on academic wise?' He replied, 'It isn't just about academia but the whole of life, Dad.' Eventually to my relief he did focus on his studies.

Anecdotes

As related by my adult children and unchecked by me.

Timothy says:

I was a happy child. And for the first 14 months of my life, I was an only child. After that, every time mum went to Lancaster she seemed to land back home with a baby.

I have no memory of Christopher, who died

Anne, Timothy, Cherith and Andrew at Stanley Park, Blackpool

190

aged 6 weeks but what I do recall is Pastor Barrie Walton being part of our household, coming to visit before and after Christopher died, to comfort my parents. I considered Barrie and Eva to be part of our family.

We lived at Portree in Dolphinholme until I was four, when we moved into the Dolphinholme Stores. In fact, we swapped houses a few times but I don't remember doing this. I also moved schools several times. I attended Castle Secondary School for 3 ½ years, then we moved to The Hollies, Catterall so I had to go to Garstang High School for 6 months while we settled in. It took a while to sort out buses and uniforms, and when this was done I ended up at Ripley St Thomas' in Lancaster for 2 years.

I was very asthmatic. When I moved from primary to secondary school my breathing was so bad I ended up in an isolation ward in Beaumont Hospital. I suspect the change of environment hadn't helped my health. We were living above the shop. I remember sitting on the end of the bed trying to get oxygen from open window and gasping for air. Mum and Dad put one end of my bed on blocks, to raise my head and try to keep my chest clear.

I think some of our relatives were staying one bonfire night, November 5th (our parent's wedding anniversary). We were primary aged. Mum and Dad told us, 'You are going out tonight to watch the fireworks, and it will be very late, so first you have to get some sleep for a couple of hours. We'll wake you when it is time to go.' But by the time they came to get us up we were so out of it, we said, 'No, we don't want to get up' and so we stayed in bed! Whenever it was Christmas, all the family would rise early apart from me because I was a killjoy and liked my bed too much. By the afternoon everyone would be exhausted and we were all made to go back to bed for a rest.

I was primary aged when we lived at the shop, a tempting situation for young lads. Me and Andrew happily pinched bubble gum because the packs included football cards. Some years later, we confessed. I went to talk to my parents and admitted it to them. They were very forgiving and I was relieved once they knew about it. I guess being a Christian gave me the necessary guilty conscience.

I was about 10 when I decided to become a Christian and this decision still influences my life in a positive way. I've never really rebelled although I've not always plodded on as I should have done. In those days there were quite a lot of services in our chapel. One thing I hated doing – we had to take part in 'recitations' reading aloud poems or bits from the Bible. Our village even did a show - Joseph and his Amazing Technicolour Dreamcoat. 'Technicolour' doesn't come close to describing what we children had to wear! Blue sandals, colourful socks, striped shirts with bright jackets. We sang all the songs in Dolphinholme chapel and it was full to busting at the seams.

Another thing: we disposed of rubbish such as cardboard boxes from the shop, by burning it on the rec in Dolphinholme. While this was happening, Andrew and I, aged 12 or 13, liked to plant fires in the brambles. We'd snatch bits of burning paper from the fire and use them to light small patches of grass around the rec. One day the whole field caught on and went up in smoke. With the help of friends, we managed to extinguish it. It was usually a bit of fun, but that day we were petrified. Fortunately, there were no houses nearby - only the church!

As children we went with Dad to deliver groceries around the houses. Andrew and I were competitive, trying to see how fast we could do it. We'd leap out and put the bread in tins at the end of the lanes for the farm houses. In fact, we delivered bread and paraffin on the same round – you'd never get away with that today! Then at night Dad would drive a chicken wagon for someone else. He was always driving.

Sometimes Dad took us further afield. He used to drive a trailer with a container to fill up with plastic pellets at ICI Wilton near Redcar, over the A66. Andrew and I said, 'We need to go to the toilet.' But Dad passed us a pop bottle saying, 'I haven't time to stop!' Funnily enough we didn't use the bottle and the feeling of desperation wore off.

Dad would go to cattle markets to pick up cows. One of the farmers, Tom Jolly, ran a big farm near Great Eccleston. As Dad approached, Tom would shout, 'No swearing lads, preachers 'ere!' I was happy that my Dad was popular and those men were great people, the salt of the earth.

As well as his own work, Dad did his share of housework. Mum got bad migraines and she'd be off the road a lot One night at the Hollies, I came home from courting about 11pm and found Dad in the kitchen knee-deep in bubbles. He'd put fairy liquid in the dishwasher and in places it was a metre deep! We might laugh, but he was so helpful and caring for his family.

I wasn't yet qualified to drive, when I went with Dad to deliver cows from Lancaster to Glasgow. Dad should have been driving but he was too tired, so I drove. Suddenly, some plain clothes policemen passed us and pulled us in. Dad quickly said, 'Hey, let's both get out passenger side, so they don't know who is driving.' So we did. The police said, 'Don't you know the speed limit around here?' We said, 'No,' so they said, 'Right, clear off!'

I was 18 years old and by this time I had passed my test. Dad was towing my cattle wagon with a tractor unit and kept turning around to wipe the windows on the back of his cab. I kept signalling to him to look where he was going because he didn't seem to be aware. He was just being Dad!

The firm owned a little wagon which, after I passed my car test, on the 5th time, I was legally able to drive. However, I passed a far more challenging test first time: my class one HGV Straight off, I was a natural! And I still drive an HGV to this day.

Of course I didn't always listen to my conscience! In those days, we never worked on Sundays, so I clearly remember the first time I did. I drove off the motorway onto the A-road where the limit was 50mph, but I didn't slow down. I got caught doing 60mph, so I wrote a really crawling letter, explaining that the weather was dry and the traffic was very light and I was driving according to the conditions. And they let me off!

Speeding runs in the family, although I'm sure we're all more conscientious and safety aware nowadays. I once accompanied Uncle Peter to a motor show. On the way another guy overtook us so Peter put his foot down and chased him. It was Peter who got pulled up. The police said, 'We know you were racing with that other one.' Peter asked, 'What speed was I doing?' They replied, 'If we tell you what speed you were doing we will have to book you.'

1981: Just before Cherith's wedding, me and Mervyn France drove to Leicester. We gave Chez a lift back with us in the Peugeot pickup that belonged to the firm. The thing was overheating and we kept having to stop to put water in. The problem got worse and worse until it was boiling. Enough was enough, so at Charnock Richard services, we stopped to phone Dad and ask him to come and tow us home using his BMW and a rope. Dad appeared at midnight wearing his pyjamas. (He did a lot of things in his pyjamas!) He then towed us back faster than our Peugeot had gone under its own speed - about 70mph! Mervyn kept nudging me, saying, 'Flash your lights to tell him to slow down or I'm getting out!'

I was only 20 when I was delivering cattle out of Brock to Bacup, and going up the hill towards Blackburn. The police stopped me thinking I looked too young to be driving. But that wasn't the problem. The plating said you could drive a three-tonner unladen if it could carry no more than 7 tons, but this vehicle could carry ten tons. Dad had to come down to drive the truck and I had to go back in his car. For this, I had to attend court and the people there didn't really comprehend the situation, so they gave me a conditional discharge.

The following Tuesday I turned 21. That day I drove to Edinburgh with one of our drivers, Jimmy Miller. Dougie Clay then told us to go on to Newcastle to pick up his sheep. Once again we were stopped by the police. They held many counts against me, including the fact that I was still learning. Jimmy had one count, for aiding and abetting me! *(For the full story, p76)*

I was 15 when Dad and Uncle Peter bought the haulage business. The biggest disappointment I ever had was when we got news that our family sold it. This is how I heard the news: I was getting ready to go down the road for a few days, when completely unexpectedly, Uncle Peter said, 'Tim, jump in here, I've got something to tell you.' He told me they were selling Safegard and I was devastated. It felt like a bereavement. I just wanted to go home. My parents were away somewhere, and Sheila and I were 'house-sitting' for them and that same weekend, Fulwood Free Methodist Church were using Rivendell to host an 'Alpha day'. A couple of folk, David Brewer and Joyce Parkinson, came to console me because I was heartbroken. However, hindsight is a wonderful thing and I realised later that the way the business went, they got out at the right time. And I never had to miss a single day's work because I just kept going with whichever new firm took over - Safegard were bought out by TDG, (my initials!), then Norbert Dentresangle, and now it is Expo Logistics, an American firm. I decided not to stick with Expo and moved to work for Kidds Haulage in Lancaster.

As boys, Andrew and I shared a bedroom. We had a bedside lamp with a bendy stalk and a material-type cable.

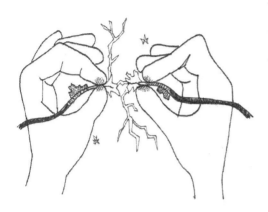

To make a longer cable, Dad had joined one piece to another using adhesive tape. 'Fiddle-fingers' Andy would fiddle with everything — everyone would move ornaments out of the way when he came into a room. The lamp was switched on and Andy had managed to unravel the adhesive tape. Suddenly Andy shouted at me to turn off the electricity. The light was flashing on, off, on, off because Andy had somehow got hold of a live wire with both thumbs and forefingers. I pulled the plug out but not before it had burnt through his fingers and he still has the scars to show for it.

One of Dad's mottos was 'Always make sure you have money in your pockets!' although he never had. Maybe he was influenced by his scouting days and learning to 'be prepared.' Come to think of it, I do remember him wearing a funny scoutmaster's hat!

Andrew says:

Dad used to believe in disciplining in anger. To my mind if we were naughty he'd whack us all first then ask questions  afterwards. As an adult I debated this with him, suggesting that discipline should come out of a clear head. Mind you we could obviously be a handful! David and Simon were in a bedroom above our parents, and Tim and I shared a room next door to it. We were too lazy or too scared to go downstairs to use the toilet during the night. So we'd just pop into our younger brothers' room to wee through a knot hole. I think we all did it! Our parents found out when they saw wee dripping into the cot in their room. The liquid was finding its way through the light fitting surround. When they stopped us from doing that, there was a header tank in the same room inside a big wooden box. Because it flushed, we believed it was refilling the toilets below, so we peed in that! But it was refilling the hot water cylinder. This meant we were always bathing in urine! Also mum always filled the kettle from the hot water because it boiled more quickly. We never got caught. How many times did she serve our guests with this 'special' tea?

Dad was always around for us, at least when the first three or four of us were very young. The nature of his work meant he was usually somewhere in the vicinity, working in the shop, or in the office at Joe Lane. He'd always let us accompany him if he was doing a run, delivering chickens or cattle or groceries. On a Saturday he'd deliver to the fell farms – as a primary aged child, I'd get up and out by 7am, aiming to be back before 9am to help him open the shop.

When we lived in Catterall we adopted an orphaned lamb. Dad had bought it from the auction for half a crown, (12 ½ p). We named him Larry. He cost us £5 per week in milk to feed him, so after about 6 months Dad took him to market. (Roast lamb, mint sauce, rosemary, garlic?) To our relief Larry was bought by a farmer who reprieved him from impending doom and took him home to be a pet for his daughter.

If we were on holiday we were allowed to go on a chicken run, which meant going to the Midlands to pick up a load of live chickens to bring to the abattoir in Garstang. Dad would struggle to stay awake as he'd worked all day. (He was trying to make money to buy himself a brand new Wolsey car.) To keep his eyes open he'd drive with his head stuck out of the window. Or he'd make us sing to him – or – wait for it – he'd light a cigarette up to keep himself awake. I was living at the shop in Dolphinholme. In the evenings we played out with our friends, games such as Tin

Can Lurky or Buzz Off. We used to hide down the ginnels behind the gardens. My strong memory is of Dad coming out to join in. He'd play games with us while no one else's dad bothered.

In terms of discipline, Dad would smack first and ask questions later. If we were scrapping, Dad would give us a smack and say, 'I'll give you something to cry for.' He could get pretty angry. Then he'd sit down and sort it out by talking. As a young preacher Dad was my first tutor. He greatly encouraged me, even giving me my first appointment at the Railway Mission in Preston, where he'd been down to preach and because he had a bad back, he suggested I went in his place. He just sent me. He taught me how to write out my sermon notes, then how to make points from them and get in the pulpit with only the points. He wouldn't let me preach from a script – and to this day I never using long-hand notes for my sermons. Dad continues to be very encouraging and supporting of me.

I never remember Dad and Peter arguing at all. But one Saturday morning I did see them fighting. We used to clean out the cattle trucks and the yard with power hoses. Dad and Pete in their green W.H. Holmes uniforms, from a great distance apart, had a massive water fight with the power hoses!

Cherith says:

I used to love going with Dad on the grocery rounds. I have fond memories of him at Christmas time going into farms with a massive bread tray full of sweets and other special things for the customers to see. They would choose their extra Christmas orders by looking at the tray display!

I was 8 years old and I asked for a transistor radio for Christmas. Suddenly Dad put a list in front of me and pointed at it to show me he had ordered a radio so I knew that I would get it. I think he was trying to reassure me, so I didn't go on and on about it to Mum.

I greatly enjoyed going with Dad on preaching appointments – mostly because I loved it when he did the children's stories. One of my favourite stories was to illustrate the Holy Spirit. Dad would put a glove on the pulpit and spoke to it. He'd say, 'Get up glove! Get up glove!' but of course it couldn't move and everyone laughed. The glove only moved after Dad put his hand into it. Of course, going with Dad also gave me one-to-one time with him, which was invaluable to me.

Dad willingly took part in the community sports' day in Dolphinholme. I remember him sitting in a wheelbarrow. He had to poke a pole through a hole but when he missed sawdust showered all over him. I loved it.

We had lovely family outings, such as picnics in various places, including the Trough of Bowland. Another adventure was to go to Blackpool Tower Circus. The end was always a wonder and amazing, because the floor mysteriously filled with water and synchronised swimmers were in it. Once, Dad arranged a coach from Dolphinholme for us and all the other villagers to see the Sound of Music in Blackpool. The coach came grandly to pick everyone up at the front of the shop. Two weeks later Dad took us again, but this time, only our family in our car. When we came out after the show, our radio had been nicked!

Dad was good at badminton; in fact, he ran a club for it. He'd take Tim, Andrew and me to badminton club at the assembly rooms in Garstang. Then Dad bought us a net on a stand so we could play badminton at home in the barn at Catterall.

I was about 7 years old when I got lost. That day, Dad was busy in the shop and Mum had a migraine. I rode away from the stores on my bike. First, I visited Hole-of-Ellel Farm to see my friend Sally Gorst at Bay Horse, then I went to the Braces at Railway Cottage at the station. Darkness fell, but on I rode to the Thorntons at Holden's

Farm where kind Mrs Thornton made me egg and chips. She asked me if everything was all right and I was nonchalant saying, 'Yes fine thanks!' It didn't occur to me the worry I was causing back home. Just as I was cycling in the dark, over the motorway bridge, Mr John Bee drove up in his Humber Imperial. He asked if I'd like to get in. I said, 'No thanks. I'll cycle home on my own.' He said, 'No you won't, because I'm part of the search party looking for you!'

At the Stores there was a junk room at the back in which was an old fashioned kitchen cupboard with pull-down door/lid. I was playing with Plasticine and pressed too hard down on this lid. The door broke and Mum went nuts.

Aged 10, I used to stay for several weeks at a time at our friends the Williamsons, who had four children. Their dad was a vet. He let me go out on his rounds with him. Once he let me watch a poodle undergoing a caesarean. Another time we climbed the embankment nearby to see a steam train - like the Railway Children!

David says:

On 24th July 1961 I was born in the Lancaster Royal Infirmary. My parents brought me home to the stores in Dolphinholme, where I lived happily until 1969 when we suddenly moved to the Hollies in Catterall. For me, aged 8, leaving Dolphinholme was traumatic. I missed my village friends and village life in general. I struggled to make new friends and tended to keep to myself. I reacted physically by becoming asthmatic. It didn't help when I moved from Bilsborough Primary School to Ripley Secondary School, a further trek from home. Our parents were so busy it would have been almost impossible for them to taxi us to the homes of school friends. However, I did have some very good friends at church: Tom Whitaker, Dave Sudell and Bob Hardman. The four of us hung around together, otherwise I tended to stay at home.

My primary memories are as you'd expect, all about trucks – what else? As a lad, I remember going out with Dad at night to pick up broiler hens up for FMC. (No, FMC is not the 'Free Methodist Church!' – it's a chicken factory at Garstang.) Dad would load all the chickens and climb back into the driver's seat with his arms all red, totally scratched up from their sharp claws and beaks. When we lived in Catterall, we'd often wait in to find out what time the cattle would be released from lairage in Birkenhead. (Lairage is where cattle are rested before moving on to market or to the slaughterhouse). Then at about 3pm we'd go to collect the cattle and deliver them to York. I remember being at school and being able to recite from memory every town en route from Birkenhead to York ending 'Ikley, Otley, Harewood, Tadcaster, York.'

Apart from the odd trip to market, my main memories of Dad were from holidays. We always went to Cornwall in the Caravette, every nook and cranny of which would be stuffed with Mum's baking, shortbread, apple slices, flapjack and so on, all strictly rationed of course! The journey was so long in those days, with no M5, that we'd have to stop overnight in a layby in Okehampton to sleep. The Caravette was a massive vehicle but imagine the scene; Simon and Jonny in the front double bed, Andrew and Chez in the overhead, Tim on a camp-bed in the aisle, and finally, Mum and Dad in a double bed at the back. One of the best things we did on holiday was to spend two whole day's budget on a bright orange Campari dinghy. What happened to the Caravette in the end? I think Aunty Betty wrote it off in an accident somewhere in Gloucester.

Talking of Aunty Betty - I remember, aged 7, playing in the lifts at Top Rank near the Lancaster turn off. We kids used to walk a mile or so just to play in the lifts of a motorway service station! Aunty Betty used to work there. When she was on duty she'd give us a discount off food.

Even better, Betty's friend (a rough lass from Catterall) used to give us food for free! Usually chips.

Mum worked hard, often resulting in her having bad migraines. She'd take to her bed for a few days at a time. Andy would step into the breach and look after us all, especially Jonny and Jason when they were babies. Through my teenage years I felt close to Andy, looking up to him. And because he could drive, he'd take me about quite a lot, usually to youth gatherings at the Free Methodist Church in Garstang. Here, Phil and Audrey Talbot were my first youth workers, succeeded by Alec and Christine Sayer, who are now parents-in-law to my daughter Alex. And for those of you who know them, Tom and Barbara Stackhouse were going out with each other.

As a young person, I never rebelled from church. In fact, I genuinely enjoyed it. For a long time, Dad was the 'Sunday School Superintendent' – leading to a strange family habit – we would eat our Sunday roast at on a Saturday dinner time (mid-day). Church was a major part of all our lives. We were brought up 'ascend the mountain before you can take part' but I didn't rebel from this. We would go to Hollybush and camp there. When I was 13 I had an experience of being filled with the Holy Spirit. It was real. I felt strong and full of faith. It was at Hollybush we met the Hardman family from Inglewhite. They moved from Inglewhite to Garstang and joined our church.

As a boy I had four hamsters all called Hammy, who met a variety of dreadful endings. However, I'm sure one never died - most likely he's still alive somewhere under the floorboards. Then our cousin Matthew had an Old

English sheepdog that I *think* was called Patch. Matthew couldn't keep him and gave him to our family. I loved him very much, but knowing me, I probably didn't walk him enough. We kept Patch in the coal shed. One day, he 'disappeared' and is now with the doggies in the sky.

If I did get in trouble as a lad, it could be for talking back at Mum. As siblings we naturally fought among ourselves; once I picked on Simon for a reason I've forgotten, and Andrew punched me in the face and knocked me to the floor. There was an unspoken pecking order between all of us. Cherith, being the only girl, was never listened to.

I worked for the firm. I left Ripley school and started work – but I was doing a milk-round two mornings a week and on Thursdays, Fridays and Saturdays I worked in Booths, stacking fruit and veg shelves. Aged 15 I worked for W.H. Holmes. Before I was 16 I left school to work for the firm. Only one month later, I rolled the forklift over and smashed my foot. *(See Accidents p178)*

The others all thought I wanted to be an only child! This stems from me going, by myself, to stay with Mum's cousin, Aunty Rita. (The daughter of Nana Phillips' sister) Rita's only child was Valerie. I've no idea why I was the only one who would stay there. Aunty Rita spoilt me rotten and I quickly got used to the special attention!

Andy taught me to drive. Aged 17, I past my test in a mini countryman. This opened up a new and different world to me. On Friday nights I'd drive (alone) to Bradford to watch stock cars. I felt amazing and free doing this. I never met anyone else there, because I was content to watch the rallies, then go home. I started rally driving, and for the first time I made friends outside of church. I consider myself to be fairly antisocial; Jayne and I are probably similar to Dad and Mum, being happy just with each other.

The year before Jayne and I married, our family moved to Haverhill. I've no idea why, but my main memory of that time is how much Mum looked after me during that year; washing, ironing, making my bed. I had a room to myself for the first time. This fact stands out in my mind and I don't know why.

Simon says:

The fifth child! I was born in 1965, so I was 4 when Dad and Peter bought the business in 1969. Our parents sold things to pay for the business so it cost them a lot. I remember going around jumble sales with mum looking for clothes. We also had hand-me-downs from other families. I'm laughing (a little!) thinking of Andrew wearing green 'bags' with a white tank-top and a striped shirt. Oh, and platform shoes! We were teenagers when Mum bought Dave a purple jacket that he refused to wear, so Mr Compliant wore it. Yes, that's me! When I went to high school, (Ripley) I had *Bobby Shafto* buckles on my shoes. I also wore Cherith's jeans, which actually were okay and no one noticed, but the zip was on the wrong side and *I* knew I was wearing girl's jeans.

When I was an infant, Andrew, David and I were in the bath above the store in Dolphinholme. It was full of bubbles that went up and up and up. My brothers pulled me down so I was under the bubble mountain. It was frightening and I got a bit of a bubble phobia because of it.

We generally bullied one another, mostly name calling and thumping. We were horrid to Jonny, calling him 'Jonny BooBoo,' even though I doubt he cried any more than the rest of us. Jason was 'Big Ears' and Tim 'Grandad.' We teased Tim because we thought he was grumpy and when he was only a teenager he played the music of Jim Reeves and Slim Whitman. (Now I'm older I can say that Jim Reeves has a pretty good voice!) We also tried playing monopoly. Once all my brothers ganged up against me to beat me and bankrupt me. I got so mad I chucked the monopoly board in the air.

Dad regularly took us to the cinema. We saw the flop of The Lord of the Rings before the Peter Jackson's brilliant version. It was meant to be a new thing, filmed as live action with animation on top! Critics panned it. Again, Dad took us to the cinema just after Andrew had stuffed VCK16R, a giant, blue Crown Toyota – so we went in Mum's new car – it was her first ever brand new car, a Peugeot 305, light green with a brown vinyl roof. We saw The Ten commandments at Morecambe Empire Theatre. Afterwards Dad took us out for a proper Chinese meal. I ordered a Chinese tea which tasted of perfume, so Andrew drank it. I had chicken soup and it was really thin with sweetcorn and chicken floating in it.

*

Even if you moved your head slightly when Grandad Gardner (Harold) was combing your hair, he'd turn the brush over and whack our heads. He'd done the same to Dad when he was a lad. Like many parents of that generation, discipline meant 'whack first, talk later.' Sometimes he got it right – for example, when I was ten years old, we were doing the usual 'Saturday gardening' and the usual winding each other up. I became so frustrated with Jonny that I threw a three-pronged rake at him. Jonny ducked and the prongs hit Jason's head, drawing blood. Dad lost it! He pinned me against the glass lean-to roof and whacked me. He said I could've killed my little brother and he was right.

Other times Dad could surprise you by his fairness. There was a hen hut behind our garage. Jonny and me, with Mark Sudell and our cousin Philip were smoking behind it. Dad appeared. We quickly stamped out our cigarettes but Dad said nothing.

I'm sure the others have mentioned Dave's runt of a rabbit that he bought, the one that won second place in the summer fayre at Ripley. We couldn't believe Fluff did it until we asked Dave how many bunnies had competed. 'Two,' he told us, proudly.

Fluff came to a tragic end. We'd built a moveable cage-run so that Fluff would eat the lawn. Dad bought a collie that was wild and somehow it got Fluff. I picked up Fluff and held him in my hands and I could feel his heart going far too fast and then - the heart stopped. We buried Fluff in the mint in the garden. Other disasters: Mum ran Benji the little poodle over. Then Toby (a poodle) died - a lady came to the door and said, 'You'll need a shovel. Your dog's been run over.' Another poodle, Kim, actually lasted. Also, we had Mitsy, a ratty old poodle.

Uncle Joe and his family went to live in Germany and we ended up with cousin Pip's cat, Jemima, and their dog too. Jemima died, so mum got a new cat called Kipper to catch the mice and rats, but Kipper had asthma! Dave's cat Prudence moved with us from Dolphinholme to Catterall and promptly walked back again. It became feral.

Andrew was driving Dad and me along the little back snig to Brockholes Arms when he hit a cat. Dad made him stop to get out the wheel-brace to put it out of its misery, but it had run off and was never found.

Mum went with Andrew to the RSPCA to buy what she said would be 'a little dog.' She returned with Paddy, a massive, soppy, yellow lab. Paddy had leapt up, taken the fiver out of Andrew's hand and literally took it to reception to hand it over. So Paddy chose them. After that, Paddy followed Andrew everywhere. He'd carry huge logs which kept bumping on fence posts. Stones had to be retrieved at all costs; he'd put his head under water for ages to sniff out the right one. Once, Paddy ran after a large lump of rock that had been thrown and to our shock, he caught it in his mouth and knocked himself clean out. Thankfully he quickly recovered.

When I was 13 or 14 years old, Mum tried to marry me off to Rachel Williams. I had to go for tea with her! Then I was told there was the option of going to France with Dad in the truck so I knew what I preferred! Being in the middle of a crowd of siblings, it was great to get personal attention. I must have wanted to impress Dad because I felt a bit disappointed when at the last minute, Dad got called away and missed my Ripley School performance of the Messiah.

Dad and Mum bought Andrew a 'priceless pineapple' to use for his art A-level. It broke the bank! Then Dad complained because all Andrew did was to take one leaf off the pineapple and designed some material using that shape.

Dad worked constantly, whether at home or in the business. Once cousin Phil and I went out with Dad and Peter to do a delivery in RN700P (yes, I do remember number plates!) As we delivered the cattle the men said, 'Happy New Year!' and I realised he was working on New Year's Day.

Another time, we were in the Foden truck. I liked it because, although the steering was too light, the headlights were big. We picked up a trailer of liquid ammonia fertiliser. We were supposed to wear a mask to help you breath because the fumes off the ammonia were lethal. (The farmers injected the ammonia into the ground for fertiliser). Dad didn't wear a mask and he got dizzy and knocked the trailer to one side on its jockey wheels. Well, that is how I remember it anyway!

Jonathon says:

I was born into Dolphinholme but only lived there about 9 months before we moved house to The Hollies. The haulage business was literally in our yard. And at some point, our family life became more hectic as Nana Phillips moved in with us permanently. She had health issues. As a child I could not understand why we weren't allowed to visit her in hospital. I wasn't to know that she had died following a second leg amputation.

While the cat's away, (Dad was often away driving), I had access to all the firm's equipment that was stored in the garage. I entered into a fancy dress competition at Catterall and decided to go as a Martian. I dressed in green overalls, with pegs for antennae, and Suzie cables hanging from my back-pack with a sign saying 'Just landed.' I won first prize.

From an early age we were all able to work, something I always enjoyed. I was 9 years old when I started being paid for cleaning cars. One time, I was hoovering with a huge industrial vacuum cleaner. The top hadn't been properly fixed on. I put my hand back to switch off the machine and the top came off leaving the fan exposed. I caught my hand in the fan. Dad bandaged the wound but the next day my hand was a mess and I ended up having to go to hospital.

I loved cleaning the vans using the power hose. I must have inherited Dad's sense of humour because I remember deliberately soaking one of the drivers, Stephen Backhouse.

Another thing I liked was spending time alone. I used to walk our dogs up Joe Lane from the Hollies. I could be out for three or four hours and no one would bother about me. I thoroughly enjoyed that.

I suffered greatly from earache. It was so bad that Dad had to shove pills down me in the back room. I was in such as state that I'd refuse to accept them. Dad used to push the tablet in and hold my mouth shut until I swallowed. He was doing this out of love. The upside of the earache was I'd have appointments at Blackpool Victoria Hospital. Mum had to trail through to Blackpool, but for me it was ace because, not only could I go in the Ford Escort Ghia or the Sirocco, but I got to spend up to four hours alone with her. To get that amount of time with either of our parents was invaluable; Dad was busy and that is how it was.

Dad was also kind to us. For years I wanted a railway set of my own so Dad got me one for Christmas. He said, 'You'll not use it,' and he was right! But my favourite presents were a watch and a Trophy Five football. It was a thick football. We used it to play 'Wall-y.' We scratched marks on a wall or chucked a couple of jumpers to make a goal. If someone did a soft shot, the ball didn't bounce back well and the next player could kick it hard. It's a kind of football version of squash.

One of my best memories of Dad is of him taking me to Hobbes Music to buy an electric guitar and twelve watt Marshall amp. Dad gave me lessons with David Kellett and would take me to Lancaster for these. These guitar lessons took place near to our 'horror' dentist, Mr Hardy, who was always somehow able to hurt you. You never came out until you had cried.

I remember being bullied a lot by my older brothers. Well, that's what they tell me but, truth be told, I hardly remember being bullied at all! As an adult, Andrew apologised for treating me as 'thick!' He added, 'You are obviously far from it.'

I cherish the time we were 'forced' to go to church! I've had some good stuff in my formative years. Church was an important foundation and as an adult I've gone towards this and totally appreciate it. As a youth, I enjoyed Friday Night Club, although one night my youth leader, Glyn Marsh, took me home for fighting. I'd hit someone. Some lifelong friendships began in this church: one was Mark Mynett. (His mum Lynn used to go to the FM church.) Mark and I got into Heavy Metal Music in a big way. I had a t-shirt with the words Testament Greenhouse Effect. The design was a skull, half melted away. It looked so warped that Mum closed her eyes to iron it. (But she still ironed it!) Then when I was 16, I bought a shirt off the touts outside a gig. It had an image of Ian Gillan (the ex-lead singer of

Deep Purple) so their magic tour contained lots of magic imagery. I'd hardly got home with it when Dad saw it and decided that there were tarot cards on the image so he threw it on the fire. I don't remember my reaction but I was probably fuming.

Another person I met at church was Sarah Gibbons (who became my wife). I'd hang out with her older brother Andrew, who knew all the pubs where you could get away with drinking underage. We reckoned Mitchell's Special Brew was good stuff. At the time, it was fun to rebel.

I thoroughly hated school and was made to move down a class. Of course, I realised that to be moved down was reasonably shameful, but all the same, I nicked off Ripley a lot. I don't think I went to a games lesson for the last two years, instead we'd go to the games hall, sign in, then head down to the canal to mess about. In my heart I wanted to work because I knew what manual work was like and knew I could do it. I ended up without a single school certificate to my name.

When I left school I went straight into 'the firm' to work. I enjoyed this very much, aware that my father and uncle were highly respected locally and nationally. Then it was bought out by TDG. The men could have transferred to TDG but some left because they would miss the honest, family feel of Safegard Storage. I did work with TDG, but soon realised that doing management courses was a waste of time because I knew I'd be going to Bible College.

In 1997, I did a Lancaster and Morecambe college course in business and management. Also, I got the equivalent of a grade C English GCSE at White Cross Adult education centre. Those, plus my life experience got me as a mature student onto a degree course in Applied Theology at Moorlands College in Bournemouth. Sarah, myself and our sons moved there for this effort. I found the whole thing really hard as I struggled with being formally educated again, but in the end I got a 2:1. My Dad generously supported me throughout. Several years later (in 2014) my favourite photo is of me with Dad, taken when I received my MA Theology certificate at Nazarene College (which is affiliated to Manchester Uni.)

I was 19 years old when Rivendell happened. It was a fantastic experience to watch as Dad bought a plot and built a house with its own swimming pool. It felt amazing. We could measure our parents' success by their choice of car, from Toyota to Peugeot 504 to Audi, then Mercs and Beamers! Dad's brother and business partner moved from MGs to Porsches. Suddenly, after all the austerity we had posh holidays and good stuff. Me and Jason shared a caravan for a year, next door to our parents' mobile home. I was going out with Sarah by then. She was visiting me at the caravan when all of a sudden I began with real flu. I was so ill that Dad had to take Sarah home. I hated that!

Despite all the business, and perhaps because of it, we had some great family holidays. Going to Cornwall was a mission in itself; long journeys with so many of us crammed together in the car. Dad and Mum took Jas and me out to Mijas in Spain and it was amazing to stay in a villa with its own swimming pool.

Jason says:

Dad is warm, generous, witty, hard-nosed, the salt of the earth, impatient, forthright and a Lancs man through and through. Most of my friends from further afield when brought to my house were met with his famous words, 'Welcome to civilisation.'

Dad used various pearls of wisdom to hang his businessman's hat on. One such was the poster on the wall at Safegard reminding us, 'The customer is always king,' along with his constant reminder to 'smile' before I picked up the phone. That's what you'll still hear when you ring Dad now, the smile in the voice coupled with his positivity as he says - 'David Gardner here, how can I help you?'

It's a rare thing to have a dad who is a major hugger and who verbally tells his kids that he loves them. He's a true northerner with a hard exterior and a soft centre. My church friends told me that they used to be scared of Dad when he preached. True, at times his strong, dramatic delivery appeared to them as 'tub-thumping!' Dad might not admit to being a performer but he certainly doesn't shy away from the limelight, so it's not surprising that most of his kids are confident enough to step onto a platform to preach, story-tell or even sing a song or two.

As the youngest Gardner child, I grew up beside Dad and Uncle Pete's fledgling haulage business. This meant Dad wasn't around much, as he worked long hours carting cattle from A to B. It was exciting for me to grow up right next to a truck yard and sheds filled with bags of sawdust which made amazing bases for army games, as long as Dad didn't catch us.

Christmases were amazing - my presents were always brilliant. Mum and Dad worked hard to give us the best. One year they gave me an overwhelming array of brand new and second-hand Action Man gear.

I remember Saturday morning chores (hard labour!) when we lived at Haverhill on Wham's Lane; Saturday, the day when the best kids' telly was on, was invariably spent stacking logs in the garage or weeding flower beds. Dad got me to unload a skip full of rubbish plywood cut-offs that he'd bought for his wood-burner and I was totally clueless about how to stack it.

I'd just passed my driving test when I crashed and wrote off two cars. I expected Dad to go ballistic, but his reaction was gracious and matter-of-fact.

During my teens I rebelled and stopped going to church. I turned my back on faith. Dad didn't preach at me but simply and quietly said, 'Don't miss out on the best, son.'

Dad's favourite way to relax was to watch late night cowboy films while guzzling whole-nut chocolate. I felt I'd literally come of age the first time he let me stay up and watch with him and he even shared a few chunks of chocolate with me.

The Final Chapter
How my life changed

At the beginning I said 'God has been,' but never more so than in this final chapter of my life. It was 2013. I'd been to church. In fact, I'd returned to Garstang Free Methodist Church, the best place I could have been in my state of bereavement, because here were my friends who had known me for years. After the service I went home. Ate lunch. Missed Anne. Out of the blue, I decided to ring up the boarding house in Perth, the one I'd stayed at while Anne was in hospital and I booked one night there. Immediately I set off driving north and arrived at 6pm. What to do next? I called in to see Geoff and Trisha Williams who lived nearby with Geoff's mum, Jean. Geoff had pastored the Free Methodist Church in Penwortham then moved to become an FM Chaplain for the NHS in Perth. Jean had been a member of the Lancaster FMC when we were pastoring there. They offered me a meal but I refused. After an hour chatting with them I went to the main street, bought fish and chips and sat in my car in a car-park eating them. I returned to Glasgow Road. The next day I drove to Fort William and stayed the night. Then the next day, Tuesday, I visited the Kyle of Lochalsh and stayed in the hotel (of the same name). That evening, dinner for one was no fun. Wednesday, I drove to Ullapool and then returned for a second night in Fort William then drove back home. I thought, 'What a complete waste of time and diesel.' I felt I'd achieved nothing.

The following year, May 2014, Andrew, Katharine and myself went on a week's holiday to Dunkeld. Whilst there they arranged to visit their friends Geoff and Trisha Williams. I went along for the ride! On the way, while discussing my lone journey to Scotland, Andrew and Katharine said, 'Why don't you ask Jean Williams if she will go with you next time?' So we arrived at Auchterader. I sat beside Jean on the settee and told her about my previous failed expedition to Western Scotland. I asked, 'Would you be interested in going with me sometime – as a companion?' She replied, 'Yes,' because she'd never seen northwest Scotland. So that was that.

Jean: I reflected later thinking 'What on earth have I done? I didn't even give it a second thought. I just said yes.' - It is out of character for me to be so impetuous.

That August, Andrew and Katharine could see I was in much the same emotional state. They said, 'Dad, why don't you do what you said and go to Scotland with Jean as your companion?' I rang Jean and asked her, 'Shall we go on that road trip?' She said, 'Yes.'

Jean: By this time, I already assumed David had had second thoughts - after all, it had been 3 months since that visit!

I said to David Jnr, 'Please find me somewhere to stay in the Kyle of Lochalsh area, and book two rooms in a hotel for three nights.' This he did, but it turned out to be forty miles north of Kyle at Talladale on Loch Marie. I confirmed this with Jean. So that September I stayed the night at the Williams' home in Auchterader. The next morning Jean and I set off for Talladale. As we drove I considered about the awkward moments of silence we'd have, because I'd been out with others on far shorter journeys than this and had to force conversation, but from the moment of setting off to the last there was never one awkward moment.

We arrived at Talladale to find we were the only guests in the hotel. Why they accepted our booking I don't know, because they said they weren't having guests as they were waiting for their daughter to have a baby and they were going to go the instant it arrived. All the same, we had a lovely time. On occasions while we were touring around, I reached across and took Jean's hand. One memorable day we were heading for Applecross, past a stretch of water. I asked Jean, 'What's the name of that isle over there?' She replied, 'Isle of Ewe.' I waited two or three minutes. Then I said, 'Do you really mean what you said?' Jean looked puzzled but nothing more was spoken.

We ate lunch in the Walled Garden café at Applecross. Whilst waiting to be served I reached across the table and took Jean's hands in mine. Yes, the hotel owner was a gourmet chef, and yes, the meals were terrific, but the overarching picture in my mind is of arriving at the meal table to see Jean sitting there looking so lovely.

Back to Auchterader. Stayed a night. Returned home to Gillows Green. Rachel and Jason were visiting. Rachel in her usual open manner sat next to me and said, 'Dad is there any romance in this?' I said, 'No, but we just clicked. We were perfectly at ease with each other.'

Jean: My daughter-in-law, Trisha, asked me if I was all right. I admitted that I felt bereft, because after this holiday with David he had more or less just driven off without a wave. It was horrible. I debated whether or not to contact him to ask if he wanted to meet me at Grange-over-Sands, because I had a planned break there with friends. My youngest son Brian became my confidant. He said, 'Go for it,' but initially I thought this would be presumptuous. Brian encouraged me (strongly!) me to do it. So I emailed David inviting him to stay. However, there was no reply. I emailed again to say, 'Forget it, I shouldn't have asked. Perhaps I've been too forward.' David rang straightaway and said, 'What are you talking about? It is in my diary.' Gradually the number of emails increased and the email subject titles evolved. The first few read 'GRANGE,' then 'YOU AND ME,' then 'US!' Over eight weeks, each heading hinted at a little bit more. My stomach was churning. I was all over the show, only able to talk to Brian. Ultimately he said,' This is worse than dealing with teenagers!'

Grange happened! At this time, I was writing these memoires with Katharine so I confided to her about my concerns that Grange only had two rooms, that it wouldn't look right if I stayed there overnight. Andrew said, 'If you don't feel comfortable, come home at the end of each day.' Jean stayed there Monday to Friday but her friends left on the Tuesday at 3pm. When I found this out I said, 'Okay then I will come up for the evening meal with you.' On the short trip up, I considered ways of getting to kiss Jean. I was deliberating what I might be bold enough to

say; 'Can I kiss you Mrs Williams?' or 'Jean, can I kiss you?'
Jean: I'd been watching out for David to arrive, to show him where to park. I met him on the carpark and leaned forward to kiss him hello on the cheek, but somehow I missed! This was probably deliberate on somebody's part!

Anyway we kissed. And that was it. We knew in that moment. I went up Wednesday and Thursday – we both knew there was only one way forward from then. Chaos reigned with phone calls during the day. Train journeys whenever I could. Stomach churnings much of the time. I said to Andrew, 'I could do without this stomach churning at 82 years of age.'
Jean: Family was the big issue. What were we going to do? How would they take this sudden news? I was sharing a house with Geoff and Trisha. David was at Gillows Green with David and Jayne. It was important to us that family should know first and quickly, but as it was – and without going into detail - the news accidentally leaked in a convoluted way.

Jean and I met every couple of weeks. In December 2014 I drove to Auchterader and proposed to Jean in her little lounge.
Jean: We'd done all this discussing and then suddenly he just asked me to marry him.

I got down on one knee, but I was close to the settee so I knew I could get up all right! The wedding was to be arranged. We couldn't get married soon enough.

When I told my sister Betty in her flat in Garstang, she stood up trembling and holding out her hands, saying, 'David, slow down! Slow down!'

We set the date for March 21st 2015. We decided to keep it simple and opted for an open family day at Garstang Free Methodist Church, with only tea and cake for a relaxed reception at church. Simon and Jason teased us; 'You're expecting us to come all that way for a cake and a cuppa?'

The wedding itself revolved around our much-loved families. Brian looked quite the gentleman as he gave his mother away. The bridesmaids were two of Jean's grand-daughters, Hannah Williams and Ellie Williams. Timothy was my best man. Simon opened the service. Andrew married us. (He often jokes about how he has married all three of his daughters and then his own dad!) Geoff gave the sermon, saying, 'These two have been married before for a combination of over 100 years, yet here they stand, ready to do it again!' Cherith and Jason read from the Bible. Rachel sang at the piano. Jonny and his son Joe were ushers along with Arran Williams. My grand-daughter, Kirsty Lamin, did the photography and she and her husband Dave made us a super photo-book of happy memories. Members of the Garstang Church cheerfully served the refreshments.

After all the excitement, Jean and I left the crowds for the HPB hotel at Askrigg near Leyburn. That evening, my children and daughter-in-laws, plus Betty, enjoyed a meal out together at The Priory in Scorton.

Jean: And Brian and Geoff took their families for a meal with their friends, the Stantons, in Garstang.

Everything takes adjusting. I was so focused on the excitement of it all that having arranged the venue, date and everything else, I'd forgotten to book the registrar first. However, just in time, I visited them, confessing, 'I know I should have come here first, but here I am, putting you last!' They kindly said, 'We'll sort you out, Mr Gardner!'

Jean: Before all this, I'd been content. I'd got my friends and church in Auchterader. David was feeling empty and at a loss. Neither he nor I had thought about re-marrying anyone. So the whole wedding thing was like a bomb going off! But throughout the months, we felt the whole thing was of God.'

I still ask myself, 'How could all this happen when Jean was 203 miles away?'

Scotland 2015

The Challenging Puzzle

Imagine a thousand-piece jigsaw puzzle rattling in its box. The picture on the box is meant to help you put things together which is time-consuming and challenging enough! But I've been relating real life, so it's been an even bigger challenge to piece things together with any degree of accuracy. My life is better being compared to a movie, with over eight decades' worth of scenes and characters shifting restlessly back and forth. So, in telling my story I've sorted out the 'edge bits' and fitted together some pieces, and hopefully as you've read this, it has sparked off your own memories, interpretations, corrections and conversations. I'm going to finish this here, because there are other things in life to be getting on with, and you all know how much I like a new project.

Nearer, still nearer, close to Thy heart,
Draw me, my Saviour—so precious Thou art!
Fold me, oh, fold me, close to Thy breast;
Shelter me safe in that haven of rest;
Shelter me safe in that haven of rest.
(Leila N. Morris 1898)

Post Script: Excerpts from my sister Betty's 1999 diary, referring to our dad, Harold's, final days

March 16th Budget day. Not good for road haulage. Fuel and tax going up. Daft because it lets lorries in from across the water, who have much cheaper rates than us.

March 28th Dad's (Harold) birthday. Simon brought his keyboard to play some of Dad's favourite hymns. Beautiful weather. Many family called.

April 16th Dad is in hospital. He has had a heart attack.

April 18th Sunday: Phone rang 7.50am. Dad very ill. I sat with him all day. Peter and I took turns in going home for a meal. David and Anne arrived home from France early. Many nephews and nieces came too.

May 12th David talked with the doctor, who did not expect Dad to pull through after his heart attack because his liver is also affected.

June 11th Dad goes into Oakfield Nursing Home. He seems to be a bit mixed up in his mind, yet he can go back years and is okay.

December 31st 1999 Our dad went to be with the Lord aged 97. (The last night of the millennium.)

A postcard showing the Dolphinholme stores before the new plate glass windows were installed by Dad.

Acknowledgements

With thanks to:

Katharine Ann Angel: for interviewing, writing, editing, proofing and publishing 'We Were Nobbut Grocers.'
I started this project by myself, but it wasn't for Katharine, it never would have been finished. Along the way we enjoyed our conversations, tears and smiles as we tried our best to put it all together. Special thanks!
www.katharineannangel.com

Mark Shotter: pen and ink illustrations

Andrew Gardner: Cover photographer

Kirsty-Jane Lamin: Cover Layout

To everyone:
family, friends,
church folk,
those I have
worked with,
laughed with,
cried with,

those who have understood my sense of humour and those to whom I need to apologise; to all whose names are mentioned herein and those whose names are not - my life is all the richer because of each one of you.

Made in the USA
Charleston, SC
26 October 2016